W9-CUG-167

FRANKLY, MY DEAR

QUIPS AND QUOTES FROM HOLLYWOOD

FRANKLY, MY DEAR

QUIPS AND QUOTES FROM HOLLYWOOD

Shelley Klein

Contents

CONTENTS

Introduction

ANDY WARHOL once said that he loved Los Angeles and he loved Hollywood. "They're beautiful," he quipped. "Everybody's plastic." In a world that favors appearance over substance, where celebrities enjoy a god-like status, and in which no one is certain whose body parts are real and whose constitute more plastic than a Barbie doll, is it any wonder that both Hollywood and those who choose to live there are viewed as a species from another planet? Treated like royalty, living in a world of ridiculous mock-Tudor houses and Olympic-sized swimming pools, the stars – and their lives – are so far removed from reality that they may as well be living on Mars.

How then, given the above, does anyone arrive at the truth of what it means to live and work in Hollywood? How do we see through the fake smiles in order to catch the real Hollywood? The answer lies with humor. In Shakespeare's plays it is always the fool who reveals the truth and, in a similar vein here, it is those who poke fun at the behemoth that is Hollywood who give us the most fruitful insights.

This collection gathers together, from Hollywood's first beginnings up to the present day, some of the most famous and infamous names in the industry, men and women such as Bette Davis, Groucho Marx, Samuel Goldwyn, Jack Nicholson, John

Huston, and Joan Crawford. Agents, producers, directors, hams and hacks, paparazzi, and media moguls – you name them, at least one of their number will be represented in this book. There is also a special place reserved for that most underrated profession of all in the Hollywood pecking order – the humble screenwriter – whose ranks have included several of America's (if not the world's) most famous names. No less than Ernest Hemingway, F. Scott Fitzgerald, and William Faulkner all at one time or another worked within the Hollywood system, for little money and even less recognition.

However, it was to be the journalists and newspaper hacks such as Ben Hecht, Herman J. Mankiewicz, and Dorothy Parker who pioneered the caustic brand of Hollywood wit. Fast, irreverent, and not infrequently bitchy, Hecht and company knew precisely how to carve up their prey. But if these legendary writers are intelligent and incisive, sadly the same cannot be said for the majority of actors who pound Hollywood's streets. Deeply insecure and highly competitive, they are by contrast far better at the bitchy aside or caustic remark than anything that could be classified as meaningful. Indeed, without writers to pen their words for them, it is hard to imagine how many actors in this volume could have functioned at all.

Finally, we come to those men and women who constitute the glue between writers and actors, and who, conveniently, like nothing better than to disparage both of those groups equally – directors and producers. "Don't ever forget what I'm going to tell you," John Huston (director of stars such as Humphrey Bogart and Katharine Hepburn) once said. "Actors are crap."

As Woody Allen pointed out, "Hollywood is not only dog eat dog, it's dog doesn't return other dog's phone calls." Thank goodness, then, for those men and women brave enough to slice through the bullshit and show us the full comic potential of Hollywood in all its star-studded and ludicrous glory.

SHELLEY KLEIN, 2005

Location, Location, Location

OF ALL the places in the world to live, Hollywood must surely rate alongside St. Tropez and Monte Carlo as one of the most glamorous and hedonistic. Yet, as the following quotes prove, all that glistens is not gold.

Hollywood is a great place to live if you happen to be an orange.

FRED ALLEN

It's not what you are in Hollywood – it's what people think you are.

ROBERT STACK

There was a very unattractive kind of snobbery about Hollywood's social life – the snobbery of Success.

DAVID NIVEN

Old Hollywood is just like desert water in Africa. Hang around long enough and every kind of animal in the world will drift in for refreshments.

WILL ROGERS

FRANKLY, MY DEAR

Everything you hear about Hollywood is true,
including the lies.

ORSON WELLES

In Beverly Hills they don't throw their garbage away,
they make it into television shows.

WOODY ALLEN

In Hollywood you can be forgotten
while you're out of the room going to the toilet.

DUSTIN HOFFMAN

There's no more drugs in Hollywood.
Health is the new drug.

SPALDING GRAY

I love Los Angeles. I love Hollywood.
They're beautiful. Everybody's plastic,
but I love plastic. I want to be plastic.

ANDY WARHOL

Living in Hollywood is like wearing fibreglass underwear –
interesting but painful.

ROBIN WILLIAMS

The true and original asshole of creation.

H.L. MENCKEN

Hollywood [is] a wondrous structure of corruption, fear, talent, and triumphs: a consortium of dream factories pumping out entertainments for millions.

DAVID NIVEN

You can take Hollywood for granted like I did, or you can dismiss it with the contempt we reserve for what we don't understand. It can be understood, too, but only dimly and in flashes. Not half a dozen men have ever been able to keep the whole equation of pictures in their heads.

F. SCOTT FITZGERALD, *The Last Tycoon*

Hollywood is a place that attracts people with massive holes in their souls.

JULIA PHILLIPS

In Hollywood, unknown actors wear sunglasses in the hope of being mistaken for knowns.

RICHARD E. GRANT

Hollywood died on me as soon as I got there.

ORSON WELLES

FRANKLY, MY DEAR

The buildings looked so fake I was amazed to see that
the façades had backs to them [. . .] It is a silly city.
JOHN BOORMAN

If I lived there, I'd *move*.
CLINT EASTWOOD *on Los Angeles*

Seventy-two suburbs in search of a city.
DOROTHY PARKER

Nobody is allowed to fail within a two-mile radius
of the Beverly Hills Hotel.
GORE VIDAL

Hollywood is a place where they place you under
contract instead of under observation.
WALTER WINCHELL

The honors Hollywood has for the writer are
as dubious as tissue-paper cufflinks.
BEN HECHT

LA weather is a sham, like most things there.
JOHN BOORMAN

LOCATION, LOCATION, LOCATION

Hollywood, land of contrasts: where any day you can
see the very rich rubbing shoulders with the rich.

KENNETH TYNAN

If you're not everything to everybody,
you're nobody in Hollywood.

ROBERT EVANS

My attitude about Hollywood is that I wouldn't walk across
the street to pull one of those executives out of the snow if
he was bleeding to death. Not unless I was paid for it.
None of them ever did me any favors.

JAMES WOODS

There are only three ages for women in Hollywood – Babe,
District Attorney, and *Driving Miss Daisy*.

GOLDIE HAWN

You can take all the sincerity in Hollywood, place it
in the navel of a fruit fly, and still have room enough left
for three caraway seeds and a producer's heart.

FRED ALLEN

Hollywood is a sewer – with service from the Ritz Carlton.

WILSON MITZNER

15

FRANKLY, MY DEAR

Hollywood didn't kill Marilyn Monroe,
it's the Marilyn Monroes who are killing Hollywood.
BILLY WILDER

Hollywood's where you spend more than you make
on things you don't need, to impress people you don't like.
KEN MURRAY

Once you lose it in Hollywood, you don't come back.
Even Jesus couldn't get resurrected in this town.
IRVING "SWIFTY" LAZAR

In Hollywood they'll forgive you if you're two-faced.
But not if you're two-chinned.
COLLEEN DEWHURST

I think that every religion says to love your neighbor.
In Hollywood they add, "But don't get caught."
ANITA EKBERG

Hollywood really knows how to blow things up,
whether it be bombs doing it to battleships or a script
accomplishing the same thing to historical fact.
LAWRENCE REED

Hollywood has no more notion of telling a story
than a blind puppy has of composing a symphony.
GEORGE BERNARD SHAW

Hollywood must be the only place on earth
where you can get fired by someone wearing
a Hawaiian shirt and a baseball cap.
STEVE MARTIN

Hollywood's a place where they'll pay you $50,000 for a kiss
and fifty cents for your soul. I know because I turned down
the first offer enough and held out for the fifty cents.
MARILYN MONROE

Hollywood's all right. It's the pictures that are bad.
ORSON WELLS

How could a New Yorker possibly take something called
the Hollywood String Quartet seriously?
LEONARD SLATKIN

I know I'm capable of creating true art through my talent
and natural artistry. But Hollywood only wants me
to show off my bust.
JAYNE MANSFIELD

FRANKLY, MY DEAR

Hollywood set out to give the people what they want.
The most horrifying thing is what people do want.
MARTIN LANE

Understand this: all the sleaze you've heard about
Hollywood? All the illiterate scumbags who scuttle down
the corridors of power? They are there, all right,
and worse than you can imagine.
WILLIAM GOLDMAN

In Hollywood, it's more acceptable for a bar owner
to possess a firearm than an ashtray.
WILL BUCKLEY

Having fun in Hollywood means running someone
around the room, preferably someone more talented
and less powerful than you.
JULIA PHILLIPS

Everyone is fiercely competitive in Hollywood.
I recall a dinner conversation with Michael Eisner in which
I mentioned that I, like Eisner, had recently undergone
bypass surgery. "Of course, mine was more serious,"
Eisner fired back.
JOHN GREGORY DUNNE

In Hollywood, the women are all peaches.
It makes one long for an apple occasionally.
SOMERSET MAUGHAM

Hollywood: ten million dollars' worth of intricate
and highly ingenious machinery, functioning elaborately
to put skin on baloney.
GEORGE JEAN NATHAN

Hollywood is where they shoot too many pictures
and not enough actors.
WALTER WINCHELL

I was also to learn that writers got drunk, actors became
paranoid, actresses pregnant, and directors uncontrollable.
Crises were a way of life in the Dream Factories: but by some
extraordinary mixture of efficiency, comprising exuberance,
gambling, shrewdness, experience, strong-arm tactics,
psychology, blackmail, kindness, integrity, good luck and
a firm belief that "the show must go on" . . . the pictures
came rolling off the end of the production lines.
DAVID NIVEN, *Bring On The Empty Horses*

Hollywood is a world with all the personality
of a paper cup.
RAYMOND CHANDLER

A dreary industrial town controlled by hoodlums of
enormous wealth, the ethical sense of a pack of jackals, and
taste so degraded that it befouled everything to touch it.

S.J. PERELMAN

Writers in Hollywood are not a tribe of Shelleys in chains,
"ruined" by movies. For the most part they are greedy hacks
and incompetent thickheads.

BEN HECHT

The people here [in Hollywood] seem to live in a little world
that shuts out the rest of the universe and everyone appears
to be faking life. The actors and writers live in fear, and
nothing, including the houses, seems permanent.

FRED ALLEN

Hollywood is a place where a man can get stabbed
in the back climbing a ladder.

WILLIAM FAULKNER

I don't go to the movies. Maybe it's the same as not eating
hot dogs after you've worked in a slaughterhouse.
You know it's all made from ears and ass parts.

HARRISON FORD

"FRANKLY, MY DEAR, I DON'T GIVE A DAMN"

Gone With the Wind, 1939

Sign Language

L ONDON has Big Ben, Paris the Eiffel Tower, Sydney the Opera House, and New York the Empire State Building. However, despite the sprawl of Los Angeles, it has no landmark buildings – rather, and uniquely, it boasts of a landmark sign, perched above the city and visible from miles around, a sign which despite its once lackluster condition is so resonant of glamour and glitz that it has become a global symbol of the entire entertainment industry.

Situated on top of Mount Lee in Beachwood Canyon, the Hollywood sign was erected in 1923 at a cost of $21,000; not, as is natural to assume, to promote the burgeoning film industry, but as a real estate billboard to advertise a property development. In his book, *Bring On The Empty Horses*, David Niven describes the scene to perfection, saying, "In Hollywood itself, a place of dusty Baroque charm, one important thoroughfare, La Cienega Boulevard, separated with great subservience on either side of an oil derrick pumping slowly like a praying mantis, and in the scrub-covered hills above, underlining its claim to fame, was a forty-foot-high wooden sign – HOLLYWOODLAND."

In the mid-1940s, the last four letters were removed to leave the now world-famous HOLLYWOOD. Soon, would-be stars and starlets were flocking to Los Angeles hoping to make it big in the film industry – some, like Marilyn Monroe, would realize their dreams, but for every success story there were countless failures, including the twenty-four-year-old Lillian Millicent "Peg" Entwistle who, having failed to ensure

herself a starring role on the silver screen, climbed up to the sign and threw herself off the letter "H" one evening in September 1932.

As if mirroring this tragedy, in the 1940s the real estate company that had erected the sign declared bankruptcy and, with the deprivations of the Second World War, the sign gradually fell into a state of disrepair. Even though the City of Los Angeles (the sign's new owners) tried to keep their property from falling down, it wasn't until the early 1970s, when the sign was awarded landmark status, that a campaign was begun to raise $250,000 for its reconstruction. Finally, in 1978, Hugh Hefner decided to open up his Playboy Mansion in a fund-raising capacity and it was at this juncture that a handful of Hollywood icons and moguls stepped in and each "adopted" a letter – at $28,000 a shot. At last, work could begin to repair the damage that had been inflicted upon it through the years, work that culminated in the "new" sign being unveiled on Hollywood's seventy-fifth anniversary before a live TV audience of approximately six million viewers.

Today, the sign remains standing tall in all of its refitted glory, and thanks to the marvels of the Internet it's not only visitors to Los Angeles who can appreciate it – webcams installed around the perimeter allow people all over the world to view LA's most prominent advertising statement twenty-four hours a day, seven days a week, three-hundred-and-sixty-five days a year.

Hollywood Sign Sponsors

Terrence Donnelly, publisher of the Hollywood *Independent Weekly*

Giovanni Mazza, Italian movie producer

Les Kelley, creator of the *Kelley Blue Book*

Gene Autry, singer

Dedicated to Hugh Hefner

Andy Williams, singer

Alice Cooper, rock singer, in honor of Groucho Marx

Warner Brothers Records

Dennis Lidtke, businessman

A Short Anecdote
Concerning Gertrude Stein

THE WRITER Gertrude Stein, on a return trip from Los Angeles to New York, was once asked about her life in Hollywood. "What was it like – out there?" the acquaintance queried.

Miss Stein didn't hesitate for a moment. "There is no 'there' out there," she boomed.

The Human Zoo

THE PHRASE "living in a goldfish bowl" is never more apposite than when referring to the lives of the celebrities who reside in Hollywood. Being a star comes at a price: lack of privacy, constant press attention, intrusive fans, prying paparazzi – it's all part and parcel of being famous. Yet, despite being among some of the richest and most privileged men and women on the planet, it is rarely, if ever, the case that celebrities appreciate the thin pane of glass separating them from their public. Here are just a few of their complaints.

Someone once said interviews are like thumbprints
on your windpipe. That's kinda how I feel.
JOHNNY DEPP

A fan came over during dinner one time and Bogey
told him to beat it. When the guy got back to his table
I heard his companion say, quite happily,
"See, I told ya he'd insult ya."
NUNNALLY JOHNSON

It's impossible to keep a secret in Hollywood.
The star tells the producer, the producer tells the hooker,
and then it goes straight to the press.
LUKE MORTON

After a while the stars believe their own publicity.
I've never met a grateful performer in the film business.
HARRY COHN

I never looked through a keyhole
without finding someone was looking back.
JUDY GARLAND

An interview for Alfred Hitchcock
was like a living autopsy.
ALEXANDER WALKER

What's awful about being famous and being an actress and
being petite is when people come up to you and touch you.
That's scary, and they just seem to think it's okay to do it,
like you're public property.
WINONA RYDER

The minute you leave your mansion,
you're doing public relations.
PAUL "PEE-WEE HERMAN" REUBENS

People living in Hollywood have to stay home if they're in a
foul mood; anything outside the home is potential publicity.
JEREMY BRETT

Hugh Grant and Liz Hurley have been going through
a bad patch, but they've decided to stay together
for the sake of the media.
FRANK SKINNER, *after the Divine Brown incident*

Ah, stardom . . . they put your name on a star in the
sidewalk on Hollywood Boulevard and you walk down and
find a pile of dog shit on it. That tells the whole story, baby.
LEE MARVIN

The paparazzi, they're the worst! They literally want
the worst to happen to you – they want to live off
your tragedy, your accident, your suicide,
your death, even.
JOAN RIVERS

There is nothing worse than being famous and broke.
KIM BASINGER

We're absolutely stupid to be embarked in a business
where our face is connected with our accomplishments.
When you get it from morning to night, it's no longer
wonderful. No dear public ever did anything for me,
and a few people in our industry have the courage to say,
"Oh, my dear public, I'd kick 'em if I could."
CARY GRANT

Being a star has made it possible for me to get insulted
in places where the average Negro could never hope
to get insulted.

SAMMY DAVIS, JR.

Any star can be devoured by human adoration,
sparkle by sparkle.

SHIRLEY TEMPLE

When you're famous people feel free to stare.
No matter where or what the situation.
And they stare as if you can't see them staring at you.
Or as if it doesn't matter!

JOHN TRAVOLTA

A celebrity is a person who works hard all his life
to become well known and then goes through back streets
wearing dark glasses to avoid being recognized.

FRED ALLEN

It's appalling, but celebrities have no secret [. . .]
My life in and 3,000 miles from Hollywood would
have been considerably easier if I'd been homosexual
inasmuch as my private relationships would then
have remained private.

REX HARRISON

There are these irresponsible people who sell addresses.
You can buy a magazine today – I'd like to go and shoot
these people myself! – with celebrities' home addresses
in it [. . .] It's a scary world.
SALLY FIELD

Why can't we avoid being followed and examined?
It is cruel to bother people who want to be left in peace.
GRETA GARBO

Some of the press are like leeches, particularly the
photographers. They never, never get enough.
They stop acting human, they want to suck you dry.
BARBRA STREISAND

The paparazzi have gotten out of hand.
If they could sell them, they would take pictures
of one micturating [urinating].
RICHARD BURTON

I'm not naturally paranoid, but you gotta watch your every
move. That, or the public does. Ever since I got arrested and
jailed for smoking pot, I get all sorts of people, and actors
sometimes, looking at me funny when I light up a cigarette
[. . .] Hell, I like to shock people, so I'm not about to quit.
ROBERT MITCHUM

THE HUMAN ZOO

Our town worships success, the bitch goddess
whose smile hides a taste for blood.

HEDDA HOPPER

I dislike the flashbulbs so much [. . .] What I have learned is,
the best way to cope with all the fuss and maintain one's
dignity is to remain quiet. Smile now and then, but stay
quiet [. . .] And you should not care *too* much what people
will think or say about you; you cannot control it anyway.

INGRID BERGMAN

I stopped signing autographs after I was asked to sign one
while standing at a urinal in a restaurant [. . .] I was already
quite cool about the idea after being asked for about the
thousandth time, "Can you remove your sunglasses so we
can see your blue eyes?" I started saying, "I'm so sorry, but
if I take off my glasses, my pants fall down." Which
doesn't deter some of them . . .

PAUL NEWMAN

The paparazzi follow me into the men's room.
"Robin, could you hold it up? Could you make the puppet
talk? Oh, you're having a movement? Oh, great! It's *Live
Stools of the Rich and Famous!*"

ROBIN WILLIAMS

The British are the worst . . . appalling. I've been really
shocked by the behavior of the British press. Richard Gere
went out to dinner with Uma Thurman. They're old friends.
Uma left the restaurant and she gets shoved up against a
railing by journalists trying to get her photograph.
She gets a cut above her eye that needed stitches.
And his driver gets stabbed in the stomach trying
to get them out. What's going on? For what?

JULIA ORMOND

I don't like to be mean to fans, but I have to have cops
around me now. The worst is when people come up
and just grab you.

JULIA ROBERTS

People follow me around, especially photographers.
They want to see who I'm with . . . like if it's another girl.
Or they'll hang around a few hours, to try and see if I'm
leaving with the person I arrived with!

DREW BARRYMORE

One thing about how the media likes to show us at our
worst is, you figure why be on best behavior all the time
when all it takes is one slip-up?

ROBERT DOWNEY, JR.

"I'M GOING TO MAKE HIM AN OFFER
HE CAN'T REFUSE"
The Godfather, 1972

Location, Location, Location

I think any girl who comes to Hollywood with sex symbol
or bombshell hanging over her has a rough road.

KIM BASINGER

Hollywood is an extraordinary kind of temporary place.

JOHN SCHLESINGER

You can't find any true closeness in Hollywood,
because everybody does the fake closeness so well.

CARRIE FISHER

Disneyland restaged by Dante.

ROBIN WILLIAMS

Take out all the homosexuals and there is no Hollywood.

ELIZABETH TAYLOR

They told me to fix my teeth, change my nose,
even get out of the business. But I stayed,
and learned and didn't give up.

LAUREN HUTTON

If only those who dream about Hollywood
knew how difficult it all is.

GRETA GARBO

My first year in Hollywood was a virtual comedy of errors.
I was told I was too tall, and too beautiful. I found myself
being cast to play dead bodies and scantily clad bimbos.

AMBER SMITH

I'm not very keen on Hollywood.
I'd rather have a nice cup of cocoa really.

NOËL COWARD

Hollywood is like life: you face it with the sum total
of your equipment.

JOAN CRAWFORD

Are we changing the idea of what beauty is? Let's hope so.
I'm not the typical Hollywood beauty. Let's hope we're
looking at the insides of people a little more.

ANNE HECHE

In Hollywood, a girl's virtue is much less important
than her hairdo.

MARILYN MONROE

I arrived in Hollywood without having my nose fixed,
my teeth capped, or my name changed.
That is very gratifying to me.

BARBRA STREISAND

The men in Hollywood? They're either married, going
through divorce, or want to do your hair.

DORIS DAY

Hollywood reporters, all day long they lie in the sun,
and when the sun goes down, they lie some more.

FRANK SINATRA

When things are going well in Hollywood,
it's absolutely delightful, if you like sycophancy.

HUGH GRANT

It's said in Hollywood that you should always forgive
your enemies – because you never know when
you'll have to work with them.

LANA TURNER

If you stay in Beverly Hills too long you become a Mercedes.

ROBERT REDFORD

The smartest, most gifted people in the world live in
Hollywood. Those who knock the town,
(1) never made it,
(2) have no chance to make it or,
(3) made it and blew it.
BILLY WILDER

Tea at the Four Seasons Hotel poolside with Kevin Kline
and a very pregnant Phoebe Cates, delineating which actors
we have worked with are definitely certifiable or psychotic
and reach a common consensus on a couple.
I have only been here forty-eight hours and can already
hear names being dropped and diarized as I plunge
Alice-like, down, down, down into Wonderland.
RICHARD E. GRANT, *With Nails*

That dreadful picture [*The Producers*]. I can't bear to watch it,
even on a small television. I'm rather sorry I did it.
I must have needed the money. Living in Hollywood
weakens ones motives.
ESTELLE WINWOOD

Hollywood gives a young girl the aura of one giant,
self-contained orgy farm; its inhabitants dedicated to
crawling into every pair of pants they can find.
VERONICA LAKE

FRANKLY, MY DEAR

If you have a vagina and an attitude in this town,
then that's a lethal combination.

SHARON STONE

In Hollywood it's not how you play the game,
it's how you place the blame.

DON SIMPSON

The most important deals in the movie industry are finalized
on the sun-drenched turf of golf courses or around turquoise
swimming pools, where the smell of barbecue sauce is borne
on gentle breezes and wafts over the stereo system
of houses that people seldom leave.

SHIRLEY MacLAINE

I don't want the Beverly Hills circuit.
I haven't got time for people who ask you how your
grandchild is and don't listen to your answer.

JERRY LEWIS

Hollywood is like a 500-pound gorilla.
What it wants for Christmas, it gets.

CHRIS KENNEDY

No one "goes Hollywood" – they were that way before they came here. Hollywood just exposed it.
RONALD REAGAN

I came out here with one suit and everybody said I looked like a bum. Twenty years later Marlon Brando came out with only a sweatshirt and the town drooled over him. That shows how much Hollywood has progressed.
HUMPHREY BOGART

When Kipling said treat failure and success the same, they are both impostors, he could not have been living in Hollywood.
LILY TOMLIN

I'll never understand the animal, the machine of Hollywood business. And I don't want to understand it. It's like joining a club, a clique just because everyone else is in it.
You don't have any particular interest in it, and it has nothing to do with who you are as a person. You just join it because it's the thing to do. The quality of life is so different in France [where Depp now lives]. There is the possibility of living a simple life. I would never contemplate raising my daughter in LA. I would never raise any child there.
JOHNNY DEPP

No one's ever happy with their position in Hollywood.
You hear that from people you'd never dream
would complain.

YASMINE BLEETH

The best actors don't seem to live in California any more.
When I went there, everyone lived in LA. Now, they don't.
Only the rocks stars and MTV people do. I don't want to live
there and become an orange.

LAUREN BACALL

I find Hollywood really toxic.

RACHEL WEISZ

This was the final dumping ground. He thought of Janvier's
Sargasso Sea. Just as that imaginary body of water was a
history of civilization in the form of a marine junkyard,
the studio lot was one in the form of a dream dump.
A Sargasso of the imagination! And the dump grew
continually, for there wasn't a dream afloat somewhere
which wouldn't sooner or later turn up on it, having first
been made photographic by plaster, canvas, lath and paint.
Many boats sink and never reach the Sargasso, but no dream
entirely disappears. Somewhere it troubles some unfortunate
person and some day, when that person has been sufficiently
troubled, it will be reproduced on the lot.

NATHANAEL WEST, *The Day of the Locust*

This is a terrible confession to make, but after I left the army
I had a number of things to try. I had a great conceit to think
that if all else failed I could always go to Hollywood.
And then I found how wrong I was.

DAVID NIVEN

When I first arrived in Hollywood, I met a studio executive
who said, "Loved your work, Joe." When I asked what
he had seen me in, he said, "Nothing."

JOSEPH FIENNES

The average Hollywood film star's ambition is to be admired
by an American, courted by an Italian, married to an
Englishman, and have a French boyfriend.

KATHARINE HEPBURN

Hollywood isn't anything like Hollywood.

WILL SMITH

Where is Hollywood located? Chiefly between the ears.
In that part of the American brain lately vacated by God.

ERICA JONG

Nobody in Hollywood is innocent.

CARY GRANT

I have noticed something that escaped me on my first film
out here: how the exact same conversational weight is given
to talk about one's nutritionist, masseur, publicist, manager,
agent, favorite eaterie and Gorby's [Gorbachev's] current
invasion of Lithuania – "D'you think there's a movie in
there?" History is mere fodder for the next picture "pitch",
and Current Affairs means which famous person is fucking
which other famous person.

RICHARD E. GRANT, *With Nails*

Why the hell don't they hire some of the old ones?
All those bastards at the studios are trying to do is find
fifty-dollar-a-week Gables, Coopers, and Bogarts.

HUMPHREY BOGART, *complaining about all the new,
young faces pouring into Hollywood*

I'm impressed with the people from Chicago.
Hollywood is hype, New York is talk, Chicago is work.

MICHAEL DOUGLAS

I don't care for the movie racket much in England,
but in Hollywood it is much worse.

NOËL COWARD

"I COULDA BEEN SOMEBODY, INSTEAD OF A BUM, WHICH IS WHAT I AM"

On the Waterfront, 1954

Some Discreet Changes to the Hollywood Sign

ALTHOUGH it is not permitted to change the Hollywood sign, over the years certain people have taken it upon themselves to "modify" the sign to read in different ways. The following are just a few examples of what has occurred.

1976 HOLLYWEED – *in response to the state of California relaxing the laws against marijuana*

1987 OLLYWOOD – *in response to Oliver North's appearance before a joint Congressional Committee to answer questions on the "Iran-Contra Affair"*

1987 HOLYWOOD – *in response to Pope John Paul II's visit to Los Angeles*

Party People

NATURALLY, with fame comes an endless round of invitations to Hollywood fund-raising events and sophisticated soirées. Some people (such as Noël Coward) loved these events, but others have been less enamored by rubbing shoulders with the glitterati.

I was the belle of the Thing and behaved ever so nicely and everyone outdid themselves to give parties and more parties and the whole thing was stinking with glamour. Our favorites were Irene Dunne, Clifton [Webb], and Gene Kelly, but I must say everyone was really mighty sweet. Joan [Crawford] gave the largest, Mrs. Calthrop on my left so we had a good time and watched the big shots disporting themselves.

NOËL COWARD, *The Life of Noël Coward,*
Cole Lesley

At my first party there (given for me), I overheard someone say, "He's the guest of honor? Who the fuck is he?"
That brought me down to earth.

MICHAEL CAINE

Parties in Hollywood are lush and so are most of the guests.

GROUCHO MARX

First I was too busy supporting myself [in Hollywood] and
then auditioning. Then when stardom hits, every daytime
hour is spent making movies, and too many night-time
hours are spent socializing, usually needlessly . . . and
nothing bores like a bad party – Barbara Stanwyck
calls them *fêtes* worse than death.

VERONICA LAKE

In my mind, I've always been an A-list Hollywood superstar.
Y'all just didn't know yet.

WILL SMITH

Everywhere I looked, there were rows of white teeth, wheat
fields of expensively coiffed hair and acres of glowing,
sun-kissed flesh. It was like walking into the pages of *Hello!*
Within seconds of arriving I spotted Tom Cruise, Nicole
Kidman, Leonardo DiCaprio, Sharon Stone, Ralph Fiennes,
Alex Kingston, Liam Neeson and Natasha Richardson –
and that was just in the bar area.

TOBY YOUNG *describing the* Vanity Fair *party
for the sixty-sixth Annual Academy Awards, in*
How to Lose Friends & Alienate People

It's just as important to see which parties you don't get
invited to. It's like a court, but not King Arthur's –
more like Richard III's.

MICHAEL CAINE

PARTY PEOPLE

I was visiting Hollywood, and I was at a party where
Shirley MacLaine was expected at any minute. The hostess
put on some rather exotic, slow music. A guest remarked,
"I can just hear Shirley now. She walks in, hears the music
and says, 'May I have the next trance?'"

DIANA DORS

All social life is now charity fund-raisers. I get fifteen letters
a day for everything from Yugoslavian dog illnesses
to marathon-runners' nipple diseases.

ANGELICA HUSTON

Hollywood parties are pretty ritzy, all right. Everything's
very pretty, you know, and the conversation can be pretty
stimulating. There's usually a lot of food for thought.
But not that much food.

RED SKELTON

There was more good acting at Hollywood parties
than ever appeared on the screen.

BETTE DAVIS

Hollywood parties? In the old days, if you didn't take
the young lady on your right upstairs between the soup
and the entrée, you were considered a homosexual.

WALTER WANGER

It's impossible to take a piss at a Hollywood bash.
There are six people in every bathroom at every party.
You have to pretend you want to do drugs
just to get into the bathroom.

JOEL SILVER

He [Alexander Korda] had forgotten how much he disliked
the big Hollywood parties, the pineapple slices on top
of the cottage cheese in the studio commissaries (though at
MGM the chicken soup with dumplings *à la* Louis B. Mayer
was excellent) and the enervating heat.

MICHAEL KORDA, *Charmed Lives*

I had to get out of Beverly Hills! I sold my home there
because I do like to drink a bit, but my neighbors were far
too health conscious. Most of them hypocrites [. . .]
We moved to Miami, where parties and drinking socially
are a way of life. In California, people drink secretly,
behind closed doors.

MICHAEL CAINE

Hollywood parties are an excuse for rich folk to have fun
and not feel guilty about it by throwing a few crumbs
to the poor.

DAN LUBECK

How to Act — Hollywood Style

ORGET Stanislawski, forget the Method — it seems that the only way to act in Hollywood is dumb, and if you think that's an exaggeration, read the following . . .

The physical labors actors have to do
wouldn't tax an embryo.
NEIL SIMON

People often become actresses because of something
they dislike about themselves: so they pretend
they are someone else.
BETTE DAVIS

Method acting? Mine involves a lot of talent,
a glass, and some cracked ice.
JOHN BARRYMORE

The most important thing in acting is sincerity.
If you can fake that, you've got it made.
GEORGE BURNS

That [Charlton] Heston is a nice guy, but what a hamola.
ALDO RAY

The whole thing is to keep working
and pretty soon they'll think you're good.
JACK NICHOLSON

I'm no actor and I have sixty-four pictures to prove it.
VICTOR MATURE

You're acting! Don't act! I don't act, that's why I'm a star.
ERROL FLYNN

Talk low, talk slow, and don't talk too f*****g much.
JOHN WAYNE

I learned to act on the big screen.
I was never a spear carrier.
I was always the star. Always.
ROB LOWE

Method actors give you a photograph.
Real actors give you an oil painting.
CHARLES LAUGHTON

I pretty much try to stay in a constant state of confusion just because of the expression it leaves on my face.

JOHNNY DEPP

Acting is standing up naked and turning around very slowly.

ROSALIND RUSSELL

Clint developed his way of talking [on the screen] by studying the breathy speech pattern of Marilyn Monroe.

SONDRA LOCKE

My honor is my work. There is none greater.

WILLIAM HURT

I really want to be a serious actress.

ANNA NICOLE SMITH

I'm a pro: I'm never late. I try to control flatulence.

DONALD SUTHERLAND

I'm so extremely intelligent that it's actually harmed my career as an actor. Actors are supposed to be cattle.

JAMES WOODS

Becoming an actor can be embarrassing. Having to cry in front of the world, or be seen naked on screen [. . .] It's also a virtual confession that you had a rotten childhood or are some kind of emotional cripple.

HENRY FONDA

I don't go for this Method-acting stuff. I'm never going to be a Meryl Streep. But then, she'll never be a Dolly Parton.

DOLLY PARTON

No one else can do what I can do. In any medium. That's what I call talent.

JACKIE GLEASON

Am I a better singer or actor? Why do people ask me that? I'm a wonderful singer! As an actor, well, judge for yourself – just don't tell me about it if you don't think I'm very good.

DEAN MARTIN

If it works, that's The Method.

JACK NICHOLSON

I don't use any particular method. I'm from the "let's pretend" school of acting.

HARRISON FORD

When I hear an actress say, "You know what,
I'm gonna have my face done, get my tits raised,
and I'm going to get another ten years out of this business,"
I say, "More power to you. Go do it."
MICHELLE PFEIFFER

The reason I'm doing Shakespeare is to see if today's
audiences can still relate to that [. . .] I'm not old or English,
or anything, so this'll prove it once and for all.
KEANU REEVES

Five stages in the life of an actor:
(1) Who's Mary Astor? (2) Get me Mary Astor.
(3) Get me a Mary Astor type. (4) Get me a young Mary
Astor. (5) Who's Mary Astor?
MARY ASTOR

You can always pick out actors by the glazed look
that comes into their eyes when the conversation
wanders away from themselves.
MICHAEL WILDING

Being an actor is always a struggle [. . .] Acting is the greatest
profession because you're dealing with yourself all the time.
It supports the self-discovery process.
KYLE MacLACHLAN

FRANKLY, MY DEAR

If you have physical attractiveness you don't have to act.
RAQUEL WELCH

Know your lines and don't bump into the furniture.
SPENCER TRACY

Listen, I got three expressions: looking left,
looking right, and looking straight ahead.
ROBERT MITCHUM

The kids keep telling me I should try this new
"method acting" but I'm too old, I'm too tired,
and I'm too talented to care.
SPENCER TRACY

Acting is largely a matter of farting about in disguises.
PETER O'TOOLE

My acting range? Left eyebrow raised, right eyebrow raised.
ROGER MOORE

I'm a whore, all actors are whores. We sell our bodies
to the highest bidder.
WILLIAM HOLDEN

I don't want actors reasoning with me about motivation and all that bull. All I want them to do is learn the goddamn lines and don't bump into each other.

JASON ROBARDS

For the most part, young actors in Hollywood are actors by default. They're morons.

MATT DAMON

To become a good actor, you have to keep watching, and if you see nothing worth copying, you'll see something to avoid.

AL PACINO

If I ever start talking to you about "my craft" or "my instrument," you have permission to shoot me point-blank.

DREW BARRYMORE

Shaw said it best: an actor can have only one great love – himself.

PETER O'TOOLE

Screenwriters

AFTER READING the following quotes from and about screenwriters, it's my guess that few Hollywood movie producers ever appreciated Shakespeare's famous line (spoken by Hamlet) ". . . the play's the thing / Wherein I'll catch the conscience of the king." The power of the written word hardly, if ever, seems to be appreciated by Hollywood bigwigs; after all, when did you last see top billing going to a screenwriter? Add to this the fact that from the 1940s onwards Hollywood has boasted writers of the caliber of Somerset Maugham, F. Scott Fitzgerald, William Saroyan, Ernest Hemingway, Christopher Isherwood, P.G. Wodehouse, H.G. Wells, Nathanael West, Clifford Odets, Raymond Chandler, Robert Sherwood, Lillian Hellman, Thornton Wilder, Thomas and Henry Mann, Bertolt Brecht, and Dorothy Parker, to name but a few, and this omission becomes even more disappointing. Ah well, roll on the next blockbuster . . .

F. Scott Fitzgerald made me think of a great sculptor who is hired to do a plumbing job. He did not know how to connect the fucking pipes so the water would flow.

BILLY WILDER

Scriptwriting is the toughest part of the whole racket, the least understood and the least noticed.

FRANK CAPRA

Let me tell you about writing for films. You finish your book.
Now, you know where the California state line is?
Well, you drive right up to that line, take your manuscript,
and pitch it across. No, on second thought, don't pitch it
across. First, let them toss the money over. *Then* you throw it
over, pick up the money, and get the hell out of there.

ERNEST HEMINGWAY

The surest way to make money in Hollywood,
judging by the shop fronts out there, is to set up a
photocopy shop Xeroxing everyone's scripts.

JOE JOSEPH

I saw that the novel, which at my maturity was the strongest
and supplest medium for conveying thought and emotion
from one human being to another, was becoming
subordinated to a mechanical and communal art that,
whether in the hands of Hollywood merchants or Russian
idealists, was capable of reflecting only the tritest thought,
the most obvious emotion.

F. SCOTT FITZGERALD, *The Crack-Up*

If the scripts were as great as the sets,
what a town Hollywood would be.

SOMERSET MAUGHAM

Good original screenplays are almost
as rare in Hollywood as virgins.

RAYMOND CHANDLER

I went out there for a thousand a week,
and I worked Monday, and I got fired Wednesday.
The guy that hired me was out of town Tuesday.

NELSON ALGREN

John Frankenheimer called up and said, "Our Japanese
actor, Toshiro, is a little shaky with his Rs and Ls. Could we
get rid of the Rs and Ls?" So I went through his dialogue
taking out as many words beginning with R and L as I could
– which is an interesting way to write a screenplay.

JOHN SAYLES

It's a scientific fact that if you stay in California,
you lose one point of IQ every year.

TRUMAN CAPOTE

If my books had been any worse I should not have
been invited to Hollywood; if they had been any better
I should not have come.

RAYMOND CHANDLER

"TOTO, I'VE GOT A FEELING WE'RE NOT IN KANSAS ANY MORE"

The Wizard of Oz, 1939

Every now and then when your life gets complicated and
the weasels start closing in, the only cure is to load up on
heinous chemicals and then drive like a bastard from
Hollywood to Las Vegas . . . with the music at top volume
and at least a pint of ether.

HUNTER S. THOMPSON

Did you hear about the starlet so dumb
that she slept with the writer?

PRODUCERS' JOKE

Not many executives actually read books in Hollywood.
Their lips get tired after ten pages.

RICHARD SYLBERT

They have followed their usual procedure and handed
my treatment over to several other people to make a
screenplay out of it. By the time they are ready to shoot
it may have been through twenty pairs of hands.
What will be left? One shudders to think.
Meanwhile, they have paid me a lot of money.

ALDOUS HUXLEY

Does she have to pray so much?
A senior studio executive to **RONALD F. MAXWELL**
with reference to his script, **Joan of Arc**

Hollywood should jettison the notion of unrealistic happy
endings. After all, Rick never got on the plane with Elsa;
Zhivago died before he was reunited with Lara;
and Wile E. Coyote never caught the Road Runner.

BOYD FARROW

My husband pulled strings and I was given fifty dollars a
week at Metro-Goldwyn-Mayer to read manuscripts and
write reports about them. In order to get the job, you had to
read two languages – or pretend that you did – and you had
to write the kind of idiot-simple report that Louis Mayer's
professional lady storyteller could make even more simple
when she told it to Mr. Mayer [. . .] It was said that if your
reports showed signs of promise you would be promoted to
what was called a junior writer position, but after that I don't
know what became of you because I was never promoted.

LILLIAN HELLMAN, *An Unfinished Woman*

Will you accept three hundred per week to work for
Paramount Pictures? All expenses paid. The three hundred
is peanuts. Millions are to be grabbed out here and your
only competition is idiots. Don't let this get around.

HERMAN J. MANKIEWICZ (*who wrote* **Citizen Kane**),
*in a telegram to journalist Ben Hecht, telling him about
Hollywood, 1925*

I get sick of those people who say if they were free of
Hollywood what they'd do. They wouldn't do anything.
It's not the pictures that are at fault, the writer is not
accustomed to money. It goes to his head and destroys him –
not pictures.

WILLIAM FAULKNER

Hollywood ruined Scott [Fitzgerald],
unless he was terribly dead before.

MARTHA GELLHORN

In Hollywood the woods are full of people that learned to
write but evidently can't read. If they could read their stuff,
they'd stop writing.

WILL ROGERS

"Do you write, Mr. Faulkner?"
"Yes, Mr. Gable. What do you do?"
Exchange between **WILLIAM FAULKNER**
and **CLARK GABLE**

You wanna be a success in this town, kid?
Just remember one thing.
No one gives a shit about the script.

LANDYN PARKER, *Hollywood screenwriter*

The executives who read the script say: "Well, the main character is not very likeable." So without changing what the main character says or does, when I introduce them, I write "Betty, a very likeable person," then they go, "Oh, these changes are wonderful! She really comes alive!" I do that all the time.

DON ROOS

That's one thing I like about Hollywood. The writer is there revealed in his ultimate corruption. He asks no praise, because his praise comes to him in the form of a salary check. In Hollywood the average writer is not young, not honest, not brave, and a bit overdressed. But he is darn good company, which book writers as a rule are not. He is better than what he writes. Most book writers are not as good.

RAYMOND CHANDLER

MGM bores me when I see them, but I don't see them much. They have been a help in getting me introductions to morticians, who are the only people worth knowing.

EVELYN WAUGH

In Hollywood, writers are considered only the first drafts of human beings.

FRANK DEFORD

The script is the literary form for a society giving up literacy.
People in Hollywood don't read them. Not even the writers
read them. They write the scenes out of order and seldom
need to scan the whole thing through except to check for
page numbers.

DAVID THOMSON

Fitzgerald? Forget it! He's nothing but trouble. I just had him
with me on location in New England and it was hopeless.
Drunk as a skunk the entire time, missing trains, getting lost,
insulting people . . . he never wrote one line I could use [. . .]
Finally I kicked him off the picture.

WALTER WANGER, *producer, as quoted in*
DAVID NIVEN's *Bring On The Empty Horses*

The Hollywood film version of my play, *Design For Living*,
retained only one line intact: "Kippers on toast."

NOËL COWARD

Giving your book to Hollywood
is like pimping your daughter.

TOM CLANCY

If she [Martha Gellhorn] does not go to Hollywood,
as she easily might, she may do good work.

The New York Times

I wrote the script for *Rocky* in three days. I'm astounded
by people who take eighteen years to write something.
That's how long it took that guy to write *Madame Bovary*.
And did that ever make the bestseller list?

SYLVESTER STALLONE

Selling my book in Hollywood I felt exactly like a merchant
selling glass beads to African natives.

HUGH WALPOLE

Martha [Gellhorn] decided to divide up the "movie element"
around her into the "good" and the "intolerable" and one
night lectured them all, after a prolonged bout of drinking,
which often made her extremely bossy, on the evils of
Hollywood for serious writers.

CAROLINE MOOREHEAD, *Martha Gellhorn – A Life*

A good script is a script to which Robert Redford has
committed himself. A bad script is a script Robert Redford
has turned down. A script that "needs work" is a script about
which Robert Redford has yet to make up his mind.

PAULINE KAEL

A schmuck with a typewriter.

JACK WARNER's *definition of a writer*

"HERE'S LOOKING AT YOU, KID"
Casablanca, 1942

A Short Anecdote Concerning Herman J. Mankiewicz

HERMAN J. MANKIEWICZ is probably best known as the writer of *Citizen Kane*, although prior to moving to California he had been a journalist for the *The New York Times*. One day, so the story goes, after Mankiewicz had moved to California to work in the film industry, he was sitting in the dining hall at Columbia Film Studios when the head of the company, Harry Cohn, walked in. After a short time, Cohn started complaining about a really awful film he'd had to sit through the previous evening, at which point one of Cohn's companions protested that while he might not have enjoyed the movie, the rest of the audience had loved it. But Cohn was having none of this nonsense. Silencing his friend he announced that he had a foolproof system for calculating the merits, or otherwise, of a film: "If my fanny squirms, it's bad. If my fanny doesn't squirm, it good. It's as simple as that." Everyone who was seated at the same table listened to this in silence, until, that is, Herman J. Mankiewicz suddenly boomed out: "Imagine, the whole world wired to Harry Cohn's ass!"

Money, Money, Money

LET'S JUST SAY that with so many stars admitting to a yearly salary equal to the GDP of a small third-world nation, King Midas would be impressed by the fortunes to be made in Hollywood. But, as Spalding Gray intimates in one of the extracts below, Tinseltown money is silly money, and not to be confused with the type of salaries the rest of us mere mortals can hope to achieve.

"We'd all like to begin by telling you that we all hope you're not one of those artists that's afraid to make money."

And I said, "Um, how much money are we talking about?"

"Well, we did the seventeen-million-dollar Stallone deal."

"S-s-seventeen? Uh, s-s-seventeen million d-dollars, right? A-all for Sylvester?"

"That's right."

I was conflicted. I didn't know whether to say "Congratulations" or "You should be shot at sunrise."

SPALDING GRAY, *Monster in a Box*

Having a lot of money is like eating popcorn.
It fills you up, but it isn't very satisfying.

TED TURNER

A man can make more money with less effort
in the movies than in any other profession.

GEORGE SANDERS

The only reason to have money is to tell any SOB
in the world to go to hell.

HUMPHREY BOGART

People will swim through shit if you put a few bob in it.

PETER SELLERS

I was twenty-one and *Platoon* had just won Best Picture
and grossed $100 million. Suddenly you're not paying
for meals or drinks. You don't drive any more.
You get success. The more money you make,
the less people want you to spend. It's very bizarre.

CHARLIE SHEEN

Money doesn't make you happy. I have $50 million,
but I was just as happy as when I had $48 million.

ARNOLD SCHWARZENEGGER

Money, money, money. Everyone has to have managers and
accountants. The entourages now! Bogie never had anyone.

LAUREN BACALL

I must have gone through $10 million during my career.
Part of the loot went for gambling, part for horses,
and part for women. The rest I spent foolishly.

GEORGE RAFT

Never in my life have I met so many unhappy men
making $100,000 a year.

WALTER WANGER (*in 1940*)

I have no bad feelings about actors getting $20 million a
picture or more. They won't give you a dime in this town
unless you can make them a dollar. No producer is going
to give anybody $20 million if he doesn't think he's
going to make much more.

ROD STEIGER

Money doesn't buy happiness.
But happiness isn't everything.

JEAN SEBERG

Hollywood, to hear some writers tell it, is the place where
they take an author's steak tartar and make cheeseburger out
of it. Upon seeing the film, they say, the author promptly
cuts his throat, bleeding to death in a pool of money.

FLETCHER KNEBEL

I've done the most unutterable rubbish, all because
of money. I didn't need it . . . the lure of the zeros
was simply too great.
RICHARD BURTON

I was like a kept woman during my twenty-one years
at MGM. You didn't need to carry money.
Your face was your credit card all over the world.
WALTER PIDGEON

The biggest reason a celebrity loses his old friends is that
unless they become celebrities too, they can't compete with
you, spending-wise. Even the few who wish to try.
GINGER ROGERS

Money gets you laid.
JACK NICHOLSON

The only reason I'm in Hollywood is that I don't have
the moral courage to refuse the money.
MARLON BRANDO

Money makes you beautiful.
MADONNA

Marlon Brando got, for an aggregate of twenty minutes
on the screen in *Superman* and *Apocalypse Now*, more money
than Clark Gable got for twenty years at MGM.
BILLY WILDER

If it's a good script I'll do it. And if it's a bad script,
and they pay me enough, I'll do it.
GEORGE BURNS

If someone's dumb enough to offer me a million dollars
to make a picture, I am certainly not dumb enough
to turn it down.
ELIZABETH TAYLOR

Hollywood money isn't money. It's congealed snow,
melts in your hand, and there you are.
DOROTHY PARKER

The bigger the budget, the bigger the heads.
It's egonomics.
BRAD LUCAS

When people say they want to be rich and famous,
just try rich and see if that doesn't get most of it for you.
BILL MURRAY

The budget for *Apocalypse Now* [in 1979] was over $25 million. For that sort of money we could have invaded somewhere.

CLINT EASTWOOD

Tinted car windows are one of the first things a celebrity buys once they become a celebrity. They're an absolute must.

WHOOPI GOLDBERG

You'd be surprised how much it costs to look this cheap.

DOLLY PARTON

The three terrible karmas are beauty, wealth, and fame – they're the things that stop you from finding true happiness.

BRAD PITT

I'm not buying a Gulfstream jet just because Arnold Schwarzenegger has one. That would be silly. I'm not that competitive or materialistic. But I bet my jet will have more special features than his . . .

TIM ALLEN

Money does buy happiness. And I'm healthy already.

MEL BROOKS

Shopping is like temporary therapy for those who are rich
and shallow, insecure, or clutter-happy.
NATALIE WOOD

The rich and famous should be treated differently.
They bring the money into Beverly Hills.
ZSA ZSA GABOR's *ninth husband,* **PRINCE FRÉDÉRIC
VON ANHALT**, *trying to explain why his wife could slap
a policeman and only go to jail for three days.*

Years ago, I saved up a million bucks from acting – a lot
of money back then – and I spent it all on a ranch outside
Tucson. Now when I go down there, I look at the place
and I realize my whole acting career adds up to
a million bucks' worth of horse shit.
ROBERT MITCHUM

The Beautiful
and the Damned

N O WOMAN likes to feel old or past her prime, but in Hollywood the need to look gorgeous twenty-four-hours a day, seven days a week, throughout your entire career means that women (in particular) are under constant pressure to defy both time and gravity.

In Hollywood there are women who spend every afternoon shopping for wrinkle-free dresses to go with their wrinkle-free faces.
SUSAN SARANDON

Hollywood always wanted me to be pretty,
but I fought for realism.
BETTE DAVIS

A woman is as old as she feels. Except in Hollywood.
LILA KEDROVA

In the movies, if you're past forty
you're practically an old crone . . .
JOAN BLONDELL

FRANKLY, MY DEAR

Sexpots age fast in Hollywood.
SHARON STONE

The secret of staying young is to live honestly,
eat slowly, and lie about your age.
LUCILLE BALL

A young leading lady is lovely but self-centred. An older
leading lady, if she still is a leading lady, is bound to be
manufactured and monstrously egotistical.
JACK WARNER

An actress must be very pretty or very talented.
In the short run, being pretty is more important . . .
IDA LUPINO

She's as beautiful as death, as seductive as sin,
and as cold as virtue.
LUIS BUÑUEL *on* **CATHERINE DENEUVE**

Like *Gone With the Wind*, [Greta] Garbo is monumentally
overrated. Her voice is deep, she has no humor, her figure
is flat, her carriage is not graceful, her feet are big,
her private life is a fog. Only her face is perfect.
ALFRED HITCHCOCK

76

I've had some plastic surgery. Anybody can look at me
and tell. But people can have too much. The trouble is,
you don't look better. So you're damned if you do
and damned if you don't. That's the bottom line.

ANGIE DICKINSON

Just recently I got asked to do a film where the guy was
exactly the same age as me and they go, "No, she's too old."

DARYL HANNAH

This business has a lot to do with sex and sex appeal.
People tend to think of sexuality as the main ingredient you
people have to offer. I beg to differ. I think older people
exude bundles of sexuality. It's just that older men and
women tend not to run around like cats and dogs in heat.

JACQUELINE BISSET

It's like a gypsy curse, it's terrible. The more famous an
actress becomes, the less she's allowed to eat. Unless she
wants to play people's mothers.

LANA TURNER

Harry Cohn once said to my face that he didn't like my
looks. I recovered my composure enough to say,
"That's all right. I'm not selling."

JUDY HOLLIDAY

TWENTIETH CENTURY FOX / LUCASFILM / THE KOBAL COLLECTION

"WHY DON'T YOU COME UP SOME TIME AND SEE ME?"

She Done Him Wrong, 1933

Dorothy in Tinseltown

IN THE 1930s Dorothy Parker reigned supreme. A leading figure of New York's famous Algonquin Round Table group, she was for many years considered the doyenne of all that was witty and clever in America. For instance, on being told that President Coolidge had died she replied, "How could they tell?"

In 1933 Parker married a much younger man named Alan Campbell, an actor turned scriptwriter who was keen to go to Hollywood and make his fortune writing movies. Together the two of them traveled west. Parker had been to LA once before when Metro-Goldwyn-Mayer had honored her with a three-month writing contract, however, as she later told a newspaper, her sojourn wasn't entirely successful:

After some weeks, I ran away. I could not stand it any more. I just sat in a cell-like office and did nothing. The life was expensive and the thousands of people I met were impossible. They never seemed to behave naturally, as if all their money gave them a wonderful background they could never stop to marvel over. I would imagine the Klondike like that – a place where people rush for gold.
DOROTHY PARKER, *You Might as Well Live – The Life and Times of Dorothy Parker*, *John Keats*

Despite her loathing of the place, Dorothy returned to Hollywood alongside her new husband in 1933 and immediately began work on a series of movie scripts that included *A Star is Born*, which was later nominated for an Academy Award. However, despite her apparent success (which included a large mansion replete with servants), Dorothy was never happy in Tinseltown, preferring instead the more intellectually challenging milieu of New York. Take, for instance, this acerbic quip she made in 1939 while addressing the left-wing Congress of American Writers:

> Out in Hollywood where the streets are paved with Goldwyn, the word "sophisticate" means, very simply, "obscene." A sophisticated story is a dirty story.

Notwithstanding this observation, during their writing partnership Dorothy and her husband made in the region of a quarter of a million dollars writing Hollywood movie scripts. Although blacklisted as a Communist for her left-wing politics, she and Alan did return one last time to write a script called *The Good Soup* that supposedly was to star Marilyn Monroe:

> We wrote a nice, little, innocent, bawdy French farce, but in this town everybody's a writer and has ideas. So they [the studio] took our script and hoked it up with dope pushers, two murders and, straight out of Fannie Hurst, the harlot with the heart of goo.

Needless to say, the script never went to production and Dorothy never put pen to paper again for the movie industry. Instead, she returned east and until her dying day remained adamantly against Tinseltown:

> I can't talk about Hollywood. It was a horror to me
> when I was there and it's a horror to look back on.
> I can't imagine how I did it. When I got away from it
> I couldn't even refer to the place by name.
> "Out there," I called it.

Silence is Golden

The movie people would have nothing to do with me until
they heard me speak in a Broadway play, then they all
wanted to sign me for the silent movies.

W.C. FIELDS

Novelty is always welcome, but talking pictures
are just a fad.

IRVING THALBERG

The silent film was not a vigorous popular art; it was a
universal language – Esperanto for the eyes.

KEVIN BROWNLOW

It would have been more logical if silent movies had grown
out of the talkies instead of the other way round.

MARY PICKFORD

I remember once seeing Garbo there and thinking
she was the most beautiful woman in the world,
and I often remember John Gilbert, whose career
was about to come to an end because his voice
shocked the talking-picture audiences . . .

LILLIAN HELLMAN

They [the Hollywood studios] are into the flavor
of the month, and that's the reality you have to live with
as an actress. Nothing you can do about it.

LAUREN BACALL

You know, when I first went into the movies Lionel
Barrymore played my grandfather. Later he played
my father and finally he played my husband.
If he had lived I'm sure I would have played his mother.
That's the way it is in Hollywood. The men get younger
and the women get older.

LILLIAN GISH

A Short Anecdote
Concerning Charlie Chaplin

COMIC GENIUS cannot easily be defined, but the following anecdote comes close to explaining why it is that Charlie Chaplin is still one of the greatest comedians of all time.

Finding himself in some difficulty over writing a silent sketch involving a fat lady slipping on a banana peel, the playwright Charles MacArthur turned to his friend Charlie Chaplin for advice.

"How, for example, could I make a fat lady, walking down Fifth Avenue, slip on a banana peel and still get a laugh? It's been done a million times [. . .] Do I show first the banana peel, then the fat lady approaching, then she slips? Or do I show the fat lady first, then the banana peel, and *then* she slips?"

"Neither," replied Chaplin. "You show the fat lady approaching; then you show the banana peel; then you show the fat lady and the banana peel together; then she steps *over* the banana peel and disappears down a manhole."

Pillow Talk

MARRIAGE *À LA* HOLLYWOOD is rarely a lasting union. In Hollywood stars leave marriage quicker than they can race up the aisle (though it has to be said Brad Pitt and Jennifer Aniston did last a grand total of four years), but perhaps this is fitting in a town where appearances are everything and substance unceremoniously spurned. Michael Jackson allegedly split with his wife, Lisa Marie Presley, having been quoted as saying that she was "invading my space," while Jackson's friend, Elizabeth Taylor, has tied the knot a grand total of seven times. And, just as Miss Taylor's marriage tally has risen year after year, so do Hollywood divorce settlements. Kevin Costner is said to have paid wife Cindy $40 million, Michael Douglas allegedly shelled out in the region of $45 million to ex-wife Diandra, and Steven Spielberg a cool $100 million to Amy Irving after their thirty-four month marriage fell apart.

But today's stars aren't exceptional when it comes to serial spouse-hopping, as the likes of five-times-hitched Lana Turner or four-times-down-the-aisle Joan Crawford could give them a run for their money. Frank Sinatra famously wed not only Nancy Barbato, but also Ava Gardner, Mia Farrow, and Barbara Marx, while Marilyn Monroe tied the knot with baseball star Joe DiMaggio (her second marriage) and eminent playwright Arthur Miller (her third) before going on to have her notorious affair with John F. Kennedy.

Summer 1968. The only man in America who was less
interested than me in sleeping with Mia Farrow was her
husband and my boss, Frank Sinatra. Theirs had to be one
of the worst, most ill-conceived celebrity marriages of all
time, and after two years of one disaster after another,
it was all over except for the paperwork.

GEORGE JACOBS *and* **WILLIAM STADIEM**,
Mr. S – The Last Word on Frank Sinatra

My sister was wailing and moping around after
her first divorce. I finally says to her, "Honey,
husbands ain't copyrighted. There's plenty more
where he came from."

MAE WEST

In Hollywood an equitable divorce settlement
means each party getting fifty per cent of publicity.

LAUREN BACALL

Here in Hollywood you can actually get a marriage licence
printed on an Etch-A-Sketch.

DENNIS MILLER

How many husbands have I had?
You mean apart from my own?

ZSA ZSA GABOR

With a second marriage, you keep your fingers crossed
and you act optimistic [. . .] Somebody did say that a
second marriage is a victory of hope over experience.
NATALIE WOOD, *speaking about her remarriage*
to **ROBERT WAGNER**

My fourth husband and I had tremendous fights.
He used his fists more than his mouth. They ought
to rewrite the ceremony: "In sickness and in hell . . ."
BETTE DAVIS

A successful man is one who can make more money
than his wife can spend. A successful woman
is one who can find such a man.
LANA TURNER

Some of the greatest love affairs I've known
have involved one actor – unassisted.
WILSON MIZNER

There's a group for men in Hollywood called Divorce
Anonymous. It works like this: if a member of the group
starts to feel the urge to divorce, they send over an
accountant to talk him out of it.
SEAN CONNERY

LUCASFILM / TWENTIETH CENTURY FOX / THE KOBAL COLLECTION

"MAY THE FORCE BE WITH YOU"

Star Wars, 1977

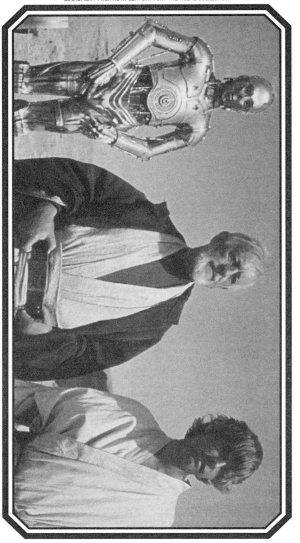

Personally I know nothing about sex,
because I've always been married.
ZSA ZSA GABOR

Gilbert Roland was a wonderful husband.
In one room of the house.
CONSTANCE BENNETT, *the former Mrs. Roland*

Why do Hollywood divorces cost so much?
Because they're worth it.
JOHNNY CARSON

In Hollywood, after you get a little success,
the next thing you usually get is a divorce.
DAN DAILEY

Marry in haste, repent in Reno.
HEDDA HOPPER

The difference between us is sex. I can take it or leave it.
But my kid brother . . . well, now, he enjoys his reputation.
Sex is the most important thing in his life. It's his hobby,
you could say.
SHIRLEY MACLAINE,
on her brother **WARREN BEATTY**

FRANKLY, MY DEAR

Alimony is proof that you pay for past mistakes.
And pay . . .
PETER O'TOOLE

My marriage license reads, "To whom it may concern."
MICKEY ROONEY, *married eight times*

God knows I love Clark, but he's the worst lay in town.
CAROLE LOMBARD, *Gable's third wife*

Yeah, I did marry beneath me. Doesn't every woman?
ROSEANNE, *on divorcing Tom Arnold*

I ought to – I married one.
GROUCHO MARX, *when asked if he knew
the definition of an extravagance.*

I wouldn't be caught dead marrying a woman
old enough to be my wife.
TONY CURTIS

In Hollywood all marriages are happy. It's trying
to live together afterward that causes the problems.
SHELLEY WINTERS

PILLOW TALK

With men it's like I'm trying every color
in the jellybean jar to see what's going to taste good.

RAQUEL WELCH

You never realize how short a month is
until you pay alimony.

JOHN BARRYMORE

Of course I married Artie Shaw.
Everybody married Artie Shaw!

AVA GARDNER

Being married to a beautiful girl is expensive.
Because you also have to hire a cook.

SAMMY DAVIS, JR.

Always a bride, never a bridesmaid.

OSCAR LEVANT, *referring to*
ELIZABETH TAYLOR*'s numerous marriages*

It's very difficult to be taken seriously when you're
introduced at a party to somebody
as the fourth Mrs. Rex Harrison.

RACHEL ROBERTS

I've only slept with the men I've been married to.
How many women can make that claim?

ELIZABETH TAYLOR

I planned on having one husband and seven children,
but it turned out the other way around.

LANA TURNER

There's only one way to have a happy marriage
and as soon as I learn what it is I'll get married again.

CLINT EASTWOOD

The trouble with some women is that they get all excited
about nothing, and then marry him.

CHER

Of course, Clark [Gable] never really *married* anyone.
A number of women married *him* . . .
he just went along with the gag.

ANONYMOUS

I should never have married, but I didn't want to live
without a man. Brought up to respect the conventions,
love had to end in marriage. I'm afraid it did.

BETTE DAVIS

PILLOW TALK

I'm not a real movie star. I've still got the same wife
I started out with twenty-eight years ago.

WILL ROGERS

In Hollywood, marriage is a success if it outlives milk.

RITA RUDNER

A husband is what's left of a sweetheart
after the nerve has been killed.

LOU COSTELLO

Marriage in Hollywood is like a nice hot bath. It's just not
that hot any more. It cools off after a short while.

JACK NICHOLSON

When I came to LA five years ago, I was shocked: all the
women dressed like hookers. And part of me was happy:
you know, I'd say to my wife [Janet Grillo, a studio executive],
"Honey, why don't you buy a pair of those pants – those
skintight *whore* pants the Brentwood housewives are wearing."

DAVID O'RUSSELL

I'm not an old-fashioned romantic. I believe in love
and marriage, but not necessarily with the same person.

JOHN TRAVOLTA

A Short Anecdote Concerning Alexander Korda and Laurence Olivier

AROUND 1940, the film producer, Alexander Korda decided to make a film about Admiral Lord Nelson and his mistress, Lady Hamilton, to be called *That Hamilton Woman*. Casting Laurence Olivier and Vivien Leigh as the two leads, everything was prepared for shooting to commence when, on walking on to the set, Korda was met with a half-dressed Olivier looking somewhat bemused. Korda asked his leading man what the problem might be, to which Olivier replied that although the costume was fine, he didn't know which arm and which eye of Nelson were supposed to be missing. Frustratingly, Korda didn't know either; in fact, nobody on the film knew the answer. Finally, someone on the set recalled that an old Hungarian actor who lived near by had once played Nelson in an operetta in Vienna. Korda immediately sent a car around to the old gentleman's house and brought him to the set where he was asked which arm and eye Nelson was lacking. The old man scratched his head and, somewhat embarrassed, said it was very difficult to remember. Korda pleaded with him to try, at which point the gentleman whispered guiltily that, truth be told, he had got rather bored with the role so each night he would swap over arms and eyes just to liven things up.

Producers and Directors

OFTEN FEARED, frequently disliked, and habitually referred to as dictators whose every command must be obeyed, producers and directors are the tough guys of the movie world.

Tales of my toughness are exaggerated.
I never killed an actor.
JOHN HUSTON

In Hollywood it's okay to be subtle,
so long as you make it obvious.
ALFRED HITCHCOCK

It's a hundred pricks against one.
WILSON MIZNER
*on describing how working for Warner Brothers
was like enjoying carnal relations with a porcupine.*

I'm overpaid, over-stimulated, over-hyped, over-age,
but I am the only person in our business who'll admit it.
JOEL SCHUMACHER

People in Hollywood are not showmen, they're maintenance men, pandering to what they think their audiences want.

TERRY GILLIAM

Most heads of studio stop reading scripts when they get their jobs and become hostage to the reports of low-paid readers, who are usually young, frustrated filmmakers.

JOHN BOORMAN

Most executives at the big studios have no guts – they're so busy holding on to their jobs they never stick their necks out. Know how [Ernst] Lubitsch found out the other day that he was no longer head of Paramount?
From his goddamn masseur!

CLARK GABLE

How did I get to Hollywood? By train.

JOHN FORD

[Hollywood] is filled with people who make adventure pictures and who have never left this place . . . religious pictures and they haven't been in a church or synagogue for years . . . pictures about love and they have never been in love – ever.

RICHARD BROOKS

96

Oliver Stone is a heavy-handed propagandist, and the women in his films make Barbie look like Sylvia Plath.

JANE HAMSHER

I deny that I ever said actors are cattle; what I said was that actors should be treated like cattle.

ALFRED HITCHCOCK

Speaking to the ladies: If you're ever approached with the line "You ought to be in pictures, I'm a producer," tell the guy to fuck off. He's a fraud, and the pictures he wants to put you in don't play in theatres.

ROBERT EVANS, *The Kid Stays in the Picture*

The first time I tried to get a movie made in the Hollywood system, my agent said to me, "There are 'yes' lists and 'no' lists, and you aren't even on the 'no' list."

ALAIN RUDOLPH

When you wake up in the morning, put on your battle fatigues, put a gun in your right pocket, and put a gun in your left pocket, and go to work. That's how you survive at the studio.

DON SIMPSON

FRANKLY, MY DEAR

I hate a man who always says yes to me.
When I say no I like a man who also says no.
SAMUEL GOLDWYN

I attribute success to having the background of just loving
the great stories of the world – and that's what makes
the most successful films – combined with my trashy,
vulgar appreciation of all that is modern Hollywood.
LESLIE DIXON

You always knew where you were with Goldwyn. Nowhere.
F. SCOTT FITZGERALD

In the court of the movie Owner, none criticized,
none doubted. And none dared speak of art. In the Owner's
mind art was a synonym for bankruptcy. The movie
Owners are the only troupe in the history of entertainment
that has never been seduced by the adventure
of the entertainment world.
BEN HECHT

This business is fuckin' crazy, the people in it even crazier.
Here I am on my knees begging a guy who delivered
a piece-of-shit script to take over everything.
They should have put me away.
ROBERT EVANS, *The Kid Stays in the Picture*

Hollywood is where everyone you meet is thinking,
"So what can you do for me?" But the Hollywood producer
is the ultimate extreme. You've probably heard the one about
the starlet who offers the producer oral sex in return for
a bit role, and he says to her, "But what's in it for me?"

ROBERT MITCHUM

Louis B. Mayer is the most written-about mogul
in Hollywood history. That's because happy reigns
have no history.

DAVID LEWIS

Hollywood today functions and is run by a small group
of people who are in adversary stances yet mostly
interchangeable: eight or nine studio heads, another
forty-odd executives, perhaps sixty top agents, a dozen
influential lawyers, as many business managers, a hundred
active producers. There are directors and stars with great
power over their own pictures, but they do not influence
the way the town is run.

JOHN BOORMAN, *Money Into Light*

PRODUCER: Would you like to play golf with me?
W.C. FIELDS: No, thanks, if I ever want to play with a
prick, I'll play with my own.

Sidney Lumet is the only director who could double-park
in front of a whorehouse. He's that fast.

PAUL NEWMAN

Hollywood has always been a cage . . .
a cage to catch our dreams.

JOHN HUSTON

Some day the bastard is going to be crushed
under one of his epics.

W.C. FIELDS *on* **CECIL B. DeMILLE**

I hired, fired, cast, produced, directed, wrote, acted, and
hyped [*Baretta*] in the media. I spent all my time trying to
bring lousy scripts to life, trying to bring mannequins
with suits on to life.

ROBERT BLAKE

He had a reputation for being difficult. While making
Full Metal Jacket, a production assistant was seen repeatedly
kicking the set and muttering, "Think of the mortgage,
think of the mortgage."

JOHN BAXTER *on* **STANLEY KUBRICK**

I was always independent, even when I had partners.

SAMUEL GOLDWYN

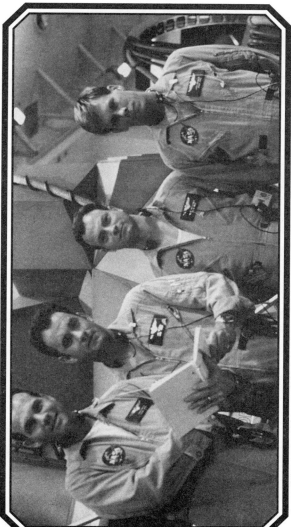

"HOUSTON, WE HAVE A PROBLEM"

Apollo 13, 1995

A Short Anecdote Concerning Jack Warner

J ACK WARNER (alongside brothers Sam, Harry, and Al) owned and ran the eponymous Warner Brothers studios not only during Hollywood's golden era (which introduced us to stars such as Jimmy Cagney, Humphrey Bogart, Bette Davis, Lauren Bacall, Errol Flynn, and Bugs Bunny), but also during its darkest period – the late 1940s, when a political blacklist was drawn up barring anyone with known (or suspected) communist sympathies from working within the film industry. It was a difficult period for everyone concerned, but David Brown, producer of movies such as *Jaws* and *The Verdict*, recalls one humorous moment when a particular director accused Jack Warner of failing to hire him because his name was on the list. Warner, according to the story, turned around and said, "There is no blacklist, and you're not on it."

Delusions of Grandeur

EGOTISM should have been a word coined especially for Hollywood stars. But who do these schmoes think they are? Actors, of course!

I'm too good to play that role.
SOPHIA LOREN
referring to a job offer to play Alexis in **Dynasty**

Why do people treat me with fun just because I am the biggest, strongest, and most beautiful man in the world?
ARNOLD SCHWARZENEGGER

I may not be as talented as some older actresses, but people keep saying how happy they are to watch me because I'm so pretty, and that's a talent in itself.
BROOKE SHIELDS

If you already know who someone is,
why on earth would you want to meet him?
EVA GABOR

Of course, *The Magnificent Seven* would have been
nothing without me.
YUL BRYNNER

I sound vain, but I could probably make a difference for
almost everyone I ever met if I chose to involve myself
with them either professionally or personally.

KEVIN COSTNER

Yeah, I've made stupid movies.
But I like my work in every film I've done.

BRUCE WILLIS

I've been planted here to be a vessel for acting,
you know what I meant?

LEONARDO DiCAPRIO

I don't make films to make friends.

DEBRA WINGER

Good-looking people turn me off. Myself included.

PATRICK SWAYZE

I can turn on the sex appeal when I wish.
I *have* it, up there [on the screen]. When I turn it on,
there isn't any man that can resist me.

KATHLEEN TURNER

I am known in parts of the world where people
have never heard of Jesus Christ.
CHARLIE CHAPLIN

Talk about Streisand, Dunaway, etc. They can be witchy
and all, but no one ever out-egoed Mae West. When she was
in London to do her play *Diamond Lil* [*She Done Him Wrong*
in the U.K.], she made all the other actresses darken their
teeth so hers would appear the whitest and brightest.
She also hired corpulent actresses for the few feminine roles,
whose primary function – as in all her vehicles, stage or
screen, American or British – was to demonstrate that
Mae West was the fairest of them all.
EVELYN LAYE

I don't mean to be a diva, but some days you wake up
and you're Barbra Streisand.
COURTNEY LOVE, *after turning up for a photography
shoot several hours late.*

Back when Charlton Heston had hair, they say
that he supposedly went to a barbershop in Hollywood
where the barber asked how he'd like his hair cut.
Charlton reportedly answered, "In complete silence."
EDWARD G. ROBINSON

If I was just normally intelligent, I could probably get away
with it, but I'm fiercely intelligent, and that's threatening.

SHARON STONE

Most people don't go to the movies, and most people
love me even if I don't have a hit movie.

GOLDIE HAWN

People think I look so fantastic.
It's like practically everyone has a crush on me.

BRAD PITT

How they could *not* give it to me was a bit of stupidity.

KIRK DOUGLAS *on not receiving an Oscar.*

When I'm working well, I like to think I'm doing
God's work.

FAYE DUNAWAY

My only regret in the theatre is that I could never
sit out front and watch me.

JOHN BARRYMORE

"SNAP OUT OF IT!"
Moonstruck, 1987

A Sarcastic Sign

"In case of an AIR RAID, go directly to RKO [a film studio]
. . . *they* haven't had a hit in years."
A sign over the entrance to Paramount Studios

Beauty and the Bitches

IF ANYONE ever considered women as being one big happy sisterhood, you only have to read the following to know that scratching each others' eyes out – and those of a few hapless men – is a far more natural scenario than loving thy neighbor.

I asked Bette Davis if she'd ever wanted to meet the Queen of England. "What for?" she snapped, "I am a queen."

NATALIE WOOD

Hollywood is full of pale imitations of Pamela Anderson and worse still, Pamela Anderson herself.

LISA MARCHANT

Gwyneth Paltrow is quite pretty in a British,
horsey sort of way.
JULIA ROBERTS

When I call my ex-husband [Lex "Tarzan" Barker] anal,
people think I'm being intellectual or Freudian. But merely
I'm using a polite word for what he really is, deep down . . .
LANA TURNER

If Cher has another facelift she'll be wearing a beard.
JENNIFER SAUNDERS

I find people in the porn world are very lively and animated.
So what if they [screw] for a living? I like a lot of them better
than the actors in Hollywood – who are the real whores,
to be perfectly honest with you.
SANDRA BERNHARD

An inveterate liar who lived in a fantasy world.
KELLY LEBROCK *on ex-husband* **STEVEN SEAGAL**

Alex Baldwin is this big new alleged sex symbol.
But he has eyes like a weasel.
He makes Clint Eastwood look like a flirt.
SANDY DENNIS

Tallulah was sitting in a group of people, giving the
monologue she always thought was conversation.

LILLIAN HELLMAN *on* **TALLULAH BANKHEAD**

Marlene Dietrich's legs may be longer,
but I have seven children.

GLORIA SWANSON

Men find it tougher to adjust to success gracefully.
They throw their weight around [and] try and make
everyone else feel less than successful.
Bruce Willis, for instance . . .

CYBILL SHEPHERD

She's the original good time that was had by all.

BETTE DAVIS *on* **MARILYN MONROE**

In Hollywood, she's revered, she gets nominated for Oscars,
but I've never heard anyone in the public or among my
friends say, "Oh, I love Winona Ryder."

JENNIFER LOPEZ

Merle Oberon speaks eighteen languages
and can't say no in any of them.

DOROTHY PARKER

Vic [Mature] can play good guy or bad guy.
Only, he can overdo the emoting. One critic said he sneers
and curls his upper lip so often, it gives the impression
he had it permanently waved.
BETTY GRABLE

All turned in and vulnerable, a child with a highly
energetic brain. From the neck up she's eighty.
SHIRLEY MacLAINE *on* **MIA FARROW**

Marion Davies has two expressions:
joy and indigestion.
DOROTHY PARKER

Dramatic art, in her opinion,
is knowing how to fill a sweater.
BETTE DAVIS *on* **JAYNE MANSFIELD**

Melanie Griffith is very sweet but dumb –
the lights are on but the dogs aren't barking.
JOAN RIVERS

Kathleen Turner's okay in stills. When she talks
and moves about, she reminds me of someone
who works in a supermarket.
ANN SOTHERN

At the RKO studios, Hepburn was called "Katharine of Arrogance." Not without reason, as I could tell you – but why bother? I really have nothing to say about Miss Hepburn which you can print.

ESTELLE WINWOOD

Miss [Elizabeth] Taylor is a spoiled, indulgent child, a blemish on public decency.

JOAN CRAWFORD

I was acting opposite Marlon Brando in *Eagle Rampant.* I asked if we could change the title because the only thing rampant about the goddamn thing was Brando's crabs.

TALLULAH BANKHEAD

She ran the gamut of emotions from A to B.

DOROTHY PARKER *on* **KATHARINE HEPBURN**

I acted vulgar. Madonna *is* vulgar.

MARLENE DIETRICH

I didn't know Judy Garland well, but after watching her in action I didn't want to know her well.

JOAN CRAWFORD

BEAUTY AND THE BITCHES

A legend in his own lifetime and in his own mind.
JENNIFER LOPEZ *on* **JACK NICHOLSON**

Frank and I were always great in bed.
The trouble usually started on the way to the bidet.
AVA GARDNER *on* **FRANK SINATRA**

No wonder Clara Bow had *It*. She caught It from receiving
too many passes from too many football players.
SUSAN HAYWARD

I always admire Katharine Hepburn's cheekbones.
More than her films.
BETTE DAVIS

I don't know anything about her except the common gossip
I heard. When it comes to men, I heard she never turns
anything down except the bedcovers.
MAE WEST *on* **JAYNE MANSFIELD**

My advice to widows – don't sell the house
and don't sleep with Frank Sinatra.
LAUREN BACALL

If I ever get hold of that hag I'll tear every hair
out of her moustache.
TALLULAH BANKHEAD *on* **BETTE DAVIS**

Marilyn Monroe was smart for only ten minutes
in her entire life. And that was the time it took her
to sign with Twentieth Century Fox.
ANNE BAXTER

"King of Hollywood?" If Clark had an inch less
he'd be called "Queen of Hollywood."
CAROLE LOMBARD *on husband* **CLARK GABLE**

Faye Dunaway says she is being haunted by my mother's
ghost. After her performance in *Mommie Dearest*,
I can understand.
CHRISTINA CRAWFORD,
JOAN CRAWFORD's *daughter*

My idea of a movie star is Joan Crawford, who can chew up
two directors and three producers before lunch.
SHELLEY WINTERS

His life was a fifty-year trespass against good taste.
LESLIE MALLORY *on* **ERROL FLYNN**

A swaggering, tough little slut.
LOUISE BROOKS
on the eleven-year-old **SHIRLEY TEMPLE**

A face unclouded by thought.
LILLIAN HELLMAN *on* **NORMA SHEARER**

I always knew Frank would end up in bed with a boy.
AVA GARDNER *on* **FRANK SINATRA**'s
marriage to **MIA FARROW**

She ought to know about close-ups.
Jesus, she was around when they invented them!
BETTE DAVIS *on* **LILLIAN GISH**

The least couth actresses I've ever worked with? [. . .]
Bette Davis and Jodie Foster.
HELEN HAYES

Take one black widow spider, cross it with a scorpion,
wean their poisonous offspring on a mixture of prussic acid
and treacle, and you'll get the honeyed sting
of Hedda Hopper.
ANONYMOUS

When I was growing up, my mother [Joan Crawford] often would say I reminded her of Norma Shearer and she'd get a strange look on her face. Only later did I realize she was pathologically jealous of Shearer.

CHRISTINA CRAWFORD

I regret that I remember not one act of kindness from her all through my childhood.

JOAN FONTAINE *on her sister* **OLIVIA DE HAVILLAND**

Darling, she's *so* distasteful.

ZSA ZSA GABOR *on* **BARBRA STREISAND**

Katharine Hepburn isn't really stand-offish.
She ignores everyone equally.

LUCILLE BALL

Equal Opportunities

Bᴜᴛ, if Hollywood women are bitches extraordinaire, then Hollywood men aren't far behind. Gentlemen, shame on you!

Mae West spoke to no one but God, Raquel [Welch] spoke only to the head of the studio, the head of the studio spoke only to God, who then relayed the message back to Mae West.

REX REED, *on the difficulties surrounding the making of* **Myra Breckinridge**

Clark Gable's ears make him look like a taxicab with both doors open.

HOWARD HUGHES

Did you hear? Heather Locklear of *Melrose Place* is taking four whole months off so she can be, she says, "a full-time mom." Isn't that *so* maternal of her?

CHRIS FARLEY

Mr. Dean appears to be wearing my last year's wardrobe and using my last year's talent.

MARLON BRANDO *on* **JAMES DEAN**

There are times when Richard Gere has the warm effect
of a wind tunnel at dawn, waiting for work, all sheen,
inner curve, and poised emptiness.
DAVID THOMSON

Lana Turner couldn't act her way out of her form-fitting
cashmeres.
TENNESSEE WILLIAMS

To the unwashed public, Joan Collins is a star.
But to those who know her, she's a commodity
who would sell her own bowel movements.
ANTHONY NEWLEY, *former husband*

She is her biggest fan. If Kathleen Turner had been a man,
I would have punched her out long ago.
BURT REYNOLDS

I hope the next time she crosses a street four blind guys
come along driving cars.
FRANK SINATRA *on his biographer,* **KITTY KELLY**

Where else but in America can a poor black boy
like Michael Jackson grow up to be a rich white woman?
RED BUTTONS

"SHOW ME THE MONEY!"
Jerry Maguire, 1992

Charlton Heston has the same problem I do. He's not likeable. Difference is, I am in real life. On the silver screen, we're both rather wooden. I can do accents – American, English – being Irish [. . .] Heston had to star in a huge hit and play some supposed kind of a saint to win an Oscar.

STEPHEN BOYD

You'd retouch until you couldn't put any more lead on the emulsion. My God, she wanted her face ironed out.

GEORGE HURRELL, *photographer,*
on **ROSALIND RUSSELL**

The more she talks, the more you begin to respect Garbo. When she had nothing more to say, she got the hell out of town. But Dietrich plunged on, sewing herself into tortuous gowns and singing the same old songs [. . .] Now she's bored, humorless, and cranky.

REX REED

Working with Cher was like being in a blender with an alligator.

PETER BOGDANOVICH

Oh, God! She looks like a chicken.

TRUMAN CAPOTE *on* **MERYL STREEP**

EQUAL OPPORTUNITIES

Were she to collide with a Mack truck,
it is the truck that would drop dead.
JOHN SIMON *on* **BARBRA STREISAND**

A venerated, self-satisfied boob.
CHARLES BICKFORD *on* **BOB HOPE**

A vacuum with nipples.
OTTO PREMINGER *on* **MARILYN MONROE**

It seems boredom is one of the great discoveries of our time.
If so, there's no question but that he must be considered
a pioneer.
LUCHINO VISCONTI
on **MICHELANGELO ANTONIONI**

His success on television is no reason for me to cast him
in a picture [. . .] He has no voice, the face is temporarily
prettier than average, and I see no great progress
since his bit in *Myra Breckinridge*.
JOHN HUSTON *on* **TOM SELLECK**

Poor Ingrid – speaks five languages and can't act
in any of them.
SIR JOHN GIELGUD *on* **INGRID BERGMAN**

We never got on. The trouble is with him [Charlton Heston],
he doesn't think he's just a hired actor, like the rest of us.
He thinks he's the entire production. He used to sit there
in the mornings and clock us in with a stopwatch.
RICHARD HARRIS

A cheap flapper who liked to get laid.
LOUIS B. MAYER *on* **JOAN CRAWFORD**

Goldie Hawn was landed with an idiot giggle, a remorseless
inclination to squeak, and, if a brain hummed behind those
dumbfounded eyes, the secret never leaked out.
DONALD ZEC

All I can say is that when I'm trying to play serious
love scenes with her, she's positioning her bottom
for the best-angle shots.
STEPHEN BOYD *on* **BRIGITTE BARDOT**

He's like a junkie, an applause junkie. Instead of growing old
gracefully or doing something with his money, be helpful,
all he does is have an anniversary with the President
looking on. He's a pathetic guy.
MARLON BRANDO *on* **BOB HOPE**

EQUAL OPPORTUNITIES

In some of his last movies, Errol Flynn had to play himself
instead of Robin Hood or Custer, etc.
Unfortunately, the role was beyond his acting abilities.
JACK WARNER

I always thought Liza Minnelli's face deserving –
of first prize in a Beagle category.
JOHN SIMON

I remember my brother once saying,
"I'd like to marry Elizabeth Taylor," and my father said,
"Don't worry, your time will come."
SPIKE MILLIGAN

Occasionally funny, usually superficial, always pompous.
BOBBY DARIN *on* **BOB HOPE**

She has only two things going for her –
a father and a mother.
JOHN SIMON *describing* **LIZA MINNELLI**
(*daughter of Vincente Minnelli and Judy Garland*).

I like Demi Moore. But that's because I have no taste.
JOE QUEENAN

123

One thing you can say about O. J. Simpson.
He never shed a drop of blood except in anger.
ROBERT MITCHUM

Judy Garland: a vibrato in search of a voice.
OSCAR LEVANT

An over-fat, flatulent, sixty-two-year-old windbag, a master
of inconsequence now masquerading as a guru, passing off
his vast limitations as pious virtues.
RICHARD HARRIS *on* **MICHAEL CAINE**

Mel Gibson in *Hamlet*? Now I've seen everything.
Except Mel Gibson's *Hamlet*.
ROBERT MITCHUM

And who can forget Mel Gibson in *Hamlet*?
Though many have tried.
HARRY ANDREWS

You have to have a stomach for ugliness to endure
Carol Kane – to say nothing of the zombie-like expressions
she mistakes for acting.
JOHN SIMON

Sylvester Stallone has a face that would look well
upon a three-toed sloth.

RUSSELL DAVIS

They've said Mayer's his own worst enemy. Well, not really.
Not while I'm around.

JACK WARNER *on* **LOUIS B. MAYER**

Over the past fifty years Bob Hope employed eighty-eight
joke writers . . . who supplied him with more than one
million gags. And he still couldn't make me laugh.

EDDIE MURPHY

I hated working with that bitch. She was the biggest bitch
in the business. Thank God I'll never have to work
with her again!

TOM BOSLEY *on* **LUCILLE BALL**

The insufferably smug and woodchuck-cheeked
Minnie Driver proffers what the French call a *tête à gifler* –
a face begging to be slapped.

JOHN SIMON

I'll never put Tom Cruise down. He's already kinda short.

DON SIMPSON

Miss Garland's figure resembles the giant economy-size
tube of toothpaste in girls' bathrooms. Squeezed
intemperately at all points, it acquires a shape that defies
definition by the most resourceful solid geometrician.

JOHN SIMON *on* **JUDY GARLAND**

I'm Number 10 [at the box office]. Right under Barbra
Streisand. Can you imagine being *under* Barbra Streisand?
Get me a bag. I may throw up.

WALTER MATTHAU

The question is whether Marilyn [Monroe] is a person at all,
or one of the greatest Dupont products ever invented.
She has breasts like granite and a brain like Swiss cheese,
full of holes.

BILLY WILDER

I love my job, and, with the exception of Kim Basinger,
most of the people I work with.

JEFFREY KATZENBERG

A celebrity endorsement doesn't change any votes . . . I don't
think that any American much cares to plumb the shallows
of Charlton Heston's mind and follow his advice.

GORE VIDAL

There's nothing I wouldn't do for Bing, and there's nothing
he wouldn't do for me. And that's the way we go through life
— doing nothing for each other.

BOB HOPE

Sinatra called Brando "Mumbles."
Brando called Sinatra "Baldie."

GEORGE JACOBS

I worked one day with her and I quit.

HENRY HATHAWAY *on* **KIM NOVAK**

I find him frightening . . . off-putting. Where some men
are self-contained, he's vacuum-packed!

ANTHONY PERKINS *on* **STEVEN SEAGAL**

I've had a few sakes, driven down Sunset, had wild fantasies
— but I didn't pull over and say, "Give me a blow job!"

PIERCE BROSNAN *on* **HUGH GRANT**

Robert Redford has turned almost alarmingly blond — he's
gone past platinum, he must be plutonium; his hair is
coordinated with his teeth.

PAULINE KAEL

A second-rate bicycle-acrobat who should have
kept his mouth shut.

KINGSLEY AMIS *on* **CHARLIE CHAPLIN**

George Sanders had a face, even in his twenties, which
looked as though he had rented it on a long lease
and had lived in it for so long he didn't want to move out.

DAVID NIVEN

There have been times when I've been ashamed to take the
money. But then I think of some of the movies that have
given Olivier cash for his old age, and I don't feel so bad.

STEWART GRANGER

Talk about unprofessional ratfinks.

BILLY WILDER *on* **PETER SELLERS**

If Rex Harrison weren't the second-best high comedian
in the country, all he'd be fit for would be selling
second-hand cars in Great Portland Street.

NöEL COWARD

Whatever Francis [Ford Coppola] does for you
always ends up benefiting Francis most.

GEORGE LUCAS

Own Goals

$\int$ OME PEOPLE like to wait for others to insult them, some people like to do the insulting themselves, but there is a third group – those who don't mind indulging in a spot of self-denigration. Here are just a few examples of Hollywood own goals.

I'm pure as driven slush.
TALLULAH BANKHEAD

People think I have an interesting walk.
I'm just trying to hold my stomach in.
ROBERT MITCHUM

I've done an awful lot of stuff that's a monument
to public patience.
TYRONE POWER

I have my standards. They may be low, but I have them.
BETTE MIDLER

I'm just a hair away from being a serial killer.
DENNIS HOPPER

FRANKLY, MY DEAR

I look like a duck.
MICHELLE PFEIFFER

I may not be as good as Olivier but I'm taller than he is.
ROGER MOORE

I have been known to cause diabetes in some people.
MEG RYAN

Why do I prefer prostitutes? With one of these floozies,
I don't have to pretend that I'm Clark Gable.
CLARK GABLE

I was once refused membership of a golf club because club
rules forbade actors from joining. I sent them the reviews
I got for my Bond films and was immediately allowed to join.
ROGER MOORE

I do two types of acting: loud and soft.
BING CROSBY

I have one or two temperamental outbursts a year –
each lasts six months.
TALLULAH BANKHEAD

OWN GOALS

If I have occasionally given brilliant performances
on the screen, this was entirely due to circumstances
beyond my control.

GEORGE SANDERS

I learned two things at drama school:
first, that I couldn't act; second, that it didn't matter.

WILFRED HYDE-WHITE

Cold sober I find myself absolutely fascinating!

KATHARINE HEPBURN

I'm so pretentious, I love it!

JULIE DELPY

You need to be a bit of a bastard to be a star.

LAURENCE OLIVIER

A spoiled genius from the Welsh gutter, a drunk,
a womanizer. It's rather an attractive image.

RICHARD BURTON *on himself*

I never really thought of myself as an actress.

ELIZABETH TAYLOR

"I'LL BE BACK"
The Terminator, 1984

The Hollywood Walk of Fame

You can see all the stars as you walk down
Hollywood Boulevard.
RAY DAVIES *of The Kinks, lyric to the song
"Celluloid Heroes" © Arista Records*

SECOND ONLY to the Hollywood sign as a symbol of the American entertainment industry is Hollywood Boulevard, studded with bronze plaques that mark the careers of all those of who have made Hollywood what it is today. From silent-movie actors and actresses to film directors, radio personalities, songwriters, and TV producers, the Hollywood Walk of Fame is a veritable timeline of Tinseltown's rise in eminence. The idea for the Walk began in 1960 when a total of 2,500 blank stars were first laid down, though only about 2,200 have been used so far. The first celebrity to receive a star was actress Joanne Woodward. Needless to say, some spots are better than others – the area outside Grauman's Chinese Theater is reserved for the legendary names such as Spencer Tracy, Steve McQueen, Louis Armstrong, and Tom Cruise, while lesser mortals (and dogs including Lassie and Rin Tin Tin) may find themselves relegated to a less prestigious part of the strip.

A Short Anecdote Concerning Hollywood Gossip Columnist Louella Parsons

DURING the 1930s two women ruled Tinseltown's gossip columns – Louella Parsons and Hedda Hopper. Both famously described by David Niven as being latter-day Lady Macbeths, between them Hedda Hopper and Louella Parsons boasted of having a worldwide readership of approximately 75 million. Mean, acerbic, and often relentless in her criticism, Louella could easily make or break a young actor's or actress's career, so much so, in fact, that Sam Goldwyn once quipped that "Louella is stronger than Samson. He needed two columns to bring down the house. Louella can do it with one."

The Academy Awards

I N SOME parts of the world (namely Hollywood), there is only one night of the year of any social significance – Oscar night.

Initially held just as the movies began to "talk" on May 16, 1929 in the Blossom Room at the Hollywood Roosevelt Hotel, the first Oscar for Best Film went to a World War I romance, *Wings*, while Emil Jannings narrowly beat Charlie Chaplin to win Best Actor and Janet Gaynor won Best Actress. The following year the Oscars ceremony was a little more widely appreciated, given that a Los Angeles radio station broadcast a one-hour live show of the event, and in 1953 the first TV broadcast of the increasingly popular event was shown.

These days the Oscars ceremony commands a worldwide audience of over one billion but, as these quotations testify, not everyone in Hollywood finds the Academy Awards shindig the glittering social feast it endeavors to be . . .

Two hours of sparkling entertainment
packed into a four-hour show.
JOHNNY CARSON

With the Academy Awards, if you're standing there and looking out, you're going to see many people who can't find their butt with their hand.
SEAN PENN

The Oscars are like pornography – enticing in prospect,
then boring as hell.

DAVID HARE

Nothing would disgust me more, morally, than receiving
an Oscar. I wouldn't have it in my home.

LUIS BUÑUEL

Academy Awards are like orgasms . . . only a few of us
know the feeling of having had multiple ones.

JOHN HUSTON

I would like to thank all those people who were happy
to bankroll the film as long as I wasn't in it.

GEOFFREY RUSH, *on accepting his Oscar
for Best Actor in **Shine***

I figure I made history. I'm the only nominee
who's lost twice in one night.

SIGOURNEY WEAVER

I wanted to win the Oscar so that I'd get more scripts
without other actors' coffee-stains on them.

MICHAEL CAINE

I think part of it must be my fascination with the phoniness of Hollywood. I saw Gwyneth Paltrow being interviewed – she was a few weeks away from winning her first Oscar for *Shakespeare in Love* – and she said essentially that her chief thought of the coming ceremony was to be sure to remember to wear comfortable shoes, that she had given no thought to winning and of course didn't care. Well, there aren't enough lightning bolts in heaven to cover all the falsehoods in that little discourse, but the interviewer just hung on every humble word out of little Gwyn's head.

WILLIAM GOLDMAN, *Which Lie Did I Tell? More Adventures in the Screen Trade*

It's hard to enjoy it [Oscar night] without a Valium.

DUSTIN HOFFMAN

I've overdosed on tranquilizers, so I think I'm all right.

EMMA THOMPSON

In the biz, an Oscar is better than sex.

RICHARD CORLISS

The only thing worse than not being nominated would have been to be nominated and then losing to Cher. That would have been embarrassing.

LILLIAN GISH

Oscar winners' speeches should be limited to one minute,
during which they are required by law to thank their
cosmetic surgeon and point out – with visual aids –
their most recent nips, tucks, and enlargements.

DENIS LEARY

I'll never forget the night I brought my Oscar home
and Tony [Franciosa], my husband, took one look at it
and I knew my marriage was over.

SHELLEY WINTERS

Working out the seating arrangement is tricky.
Obviously, you're going to put Jack Nicholson in a great seat,
and a facially obscure person in a less visible seat.

GIL GATES, *producer of the Academy Awards*

I hope my earrings don't fall off.
That's the only thing I'm nervous about.

SIGOURNEY WEAVER

I haven't got a chance [at winning Best Supporting Actor].
I'm up against two Orientals, one of them an amateur,
one black guy, and Sir Ralph Richardson, who's dead.

JOHN MALKOVICH (*who indeed did not win;
the Oscar went to the amateur, Dr. Haing S. Ngor*)

I thought I might win for *The Apartment* but then
Elizabeth Taylor had her tracheotomy.
SHIRLEY MACLAINE

I did sort of think I deserved an Academy Award nomination
for Catwoman [in *Batman Returns*]. But I was fully aware
that people don't ever get nominated for *Batman* movies.
I got nominated for something else that year.
MICHELLE PFEIFFER

Welcome to the Academy Awards,
or as it's known in my house, Passover.
BOB HOPE *introducing the 1978 ceremony*

Here comes Ashley Judd in her no-yeast-infection-here
Oscar gown . . .
LIBBY GELMAN-WAXNER

I'd rather watch old Doris Day movies than the Oscars.
ORSON WELLES

I don't care what they say to the press, I've never met
an actor in my life who doesn't have an acceptance speech
going through his head every day.
JANE FONDA

FRANKLY, MY DEAR

I keep my Oscars right next to the bathtub,
so I can take a bath and look at them.
What else are you going to do with them?

JODIE FOSTER

Helen Hunt won the Oscar by weighing less
than the statuette itself.

LIBBY GELMAN-WAXNER

We want to thank all of you for watching us
congratulate ourselves tonight.

WARREN BEATTY

Prayers and Polling Booths

DESPITE Arnold Schwarzenegger becoming Governor of California, and Ronald Reagan occupying the White House, Hollywood is not the first place one would think of when considering American politics. Nevertheless, the Sunshine State is as opinionated as anywhere else in the country, especially when it comes to religion and politics.

Washington comes to Hollywood only
when it wants to raise money or raise hell.

CHARLTON HESTON

Hollywood runs scared of the general public.
Fear is Hollywood's motivation; money is its goal . . .
The Hollywood movers and shakers, most of whom
should know better, go along with the pigeon-holing
depictions. We know most Jews are not racially Semitic,
as they were 2,000 and more years ago. We know most
Jews don't have so-called Jewish noses. We know there are
countless Jews with blue eyes. Hollywood knows this too.
But they still cast Germans as blue-eyed blonds – go there,
see for yourself . . . And Jews are inevitably played by
brown-eyed, dark-haired people – most typically
by Gentile actors.

SAM LEVENE

Whenever I know that an artist is trying to raise my
consciousness, I have flashbacks of Jane Fonda,
Sissy Spacek, and Jessica Lange lecturing Congress
about the realities of farm life.

BRAD HOLLAND

There is in Hollywood, as in all cultures in which gambling
is the central activity, a lowered sexual energy, an inability
to devote more than token attention to the preoccupations
of the society outside. The action is everything,
more consuming than sex, more immediate than politics;
more important always than the acquisition of money,
which is never, for the gambler, the true point
of the exercise.

JOAN DIDION

The politics of Hollywood are horrible –
it makes Washington look like *Sesame Street*.

STEVE TISCH

One thing you have to give Hollywood celebrities credit
for is their monumental gall. I mean, Barbra Streisand
insults conservatives more often than she bathes [. . .] and
Julia Roberts announces that if you look up Republican
in the dictionary, you'll find it right after reptiles . . .

BURT PRELUTSKY

There was a time, when I was working in Hollywood,
when I seriously considered getting circumcised
so I could fit in better and be more popular.
OMAR SHARIF

It was so sweet backstage – the teamsters are helping
Michael Moore into the trunk of his limo.
STEVE MARTIN, *host of the 2003 Academy Awards,
to his audience after Michael Moore had spoken out
against* **PRESIDENT GEORGE W. BUSH**.

I was banned from the Beverly Hills swimming club
because I'm Jewish. "My son's only half Jewish,"
I told them, "so could he go in up to his waist?"
GROUCHO MARX

Living on the East Coast, even being a so-called movie star
puts you on the "A" list. Combine that with being a
fashion tycoon and you end up on the "A+" list.
I never made that. A Jew never does.
ROBERT EVANS, *The Kid Stays in the Picture*

Hollywood . . . was the place where the United States
perpetrated itself as a universal dream
and put the dream into mass production.
ANGELA CARTER

Hollywood grew to be the most flourishing factory
of popular mythology since the Greeks.

ALISTAIR COOKE

Hollywood was born schizophrenic.
For seventy-five years it has been both a town
and a state of mind, an industry and an art form.

RICHARD CORLISS

Every country gets the circus it deserves.
Spain gets bullfights. Italy gets the Catholic Church.
America gets Hollywood.

ERICA JONG

Death Inc.

ＦOR ALL the glitz and glamour that Hollywood espouses, the center of the world's film industry has always had its fair share of tragedy. Though the Hollywood sign and the Hollywood Walk of Fame are both obvious landmarks, the city also harbors darker sites that attract more ghoulish visitors – houses, hotels, and streets in and upon which various celebrities have breathed their last. First and foremost among these is the Chateau Marmont – a hotel so popular with celebrities that even the corpses have been famous. But there are also other places that lure hundreds of fun-loving tourists every day of the week . . .

On Halloween night in 1993, **RIVER PHOENIX** collapsed and died outside The Viper Room, a Hollywood nightclub on Sunset Boulevard. He was only twenty-three years old.

The notorious Mafia hoodlum, **BENJAMIN "BUGSY" SIEGEL**, met his maker on June 20, 1947 at 810 Linden Drive in Beverly Hills. Bugsy was gunned down while in his sitting room reading a newspaper. Rumor had it that, having run up huge debts building the Flamingo Hotel in Las Vegas, his own childhood friends and fellow hoods Lucky Luciano and Meyer Lansky ordered the hit.

JOHN BELUSHI, star of *Animal House* and *The Blues Brothers,* died of a drugs overdose in March 1982 while staying at the famous Chateau Marmont, also located near Sunset Boulevard.

PETE DUEL, of *Alias Smith & Jones* fame, committed suicide at 2552 Glen Green Terrace in the Hollywood Hills.

MARILYN MONROE was found dead on August 5, 1962, in Brentwood, LA, after an apparent drugs overdose.

The actress and wife to Roman Polanski, **SHARON TATE**, tragically lost her life, and that of her unborn child, when Charles Manson's acolytes broke into her house and murdered her along with five friends.

1465 Capri Drive, Pacific Palisades is the location of actress **CAROLE LANDIS**'s suicide in 1948. Depressed after her affair with Rex Harrison had come to an end, Landis took a drugs overdose and was found by Harrison, but only after it was too late to save her.

They've great respect for the dead in Hollywood,
but none for the living.
ERROL FLYNN

DEATH INC.

Singer **JANIS JOPLIN** died at 7047 Franklin Avenue, in what was then known as the Landmark Hotel, on October 4, 1970. Joplin had taken a drugs overdose. She was only twenty-seven years old.

Hollywood is a town that doesn't just want you to fail,
it wants you to die.

DAVID GEFFEN

WILLIAM HOLDEN was found dead in 1981, at 535 Ocean Avenue in Santa Monica, having apparently fallen and struck his head.

Peter O'Toole looks like he's walking around
just to save the funeral expenses.

JOHN HUSTON

Ex-*Playboy* centrefold girl **DOROTHY STRATTEN** was murdered on August 14, 1980 by her husband at 10881 Clarkson Road, after he had discovered she was having an affair with the film director **PETER BOGDANOVICH**.

Photographer **HELMUT NEWTON** died in a car crash in 2004 as he was leaving the Chateau Marmont.

Hollywood obits are regularly in the high 80s – these are people who live a long time, which is what happens if you don't smoke, you work out every day, you get your body fat awesomely low, and you do only the best cocaine.

DAVID THOMSON

Interviewing celebrities is just a step above calling the morgue.

GARRISON KEILLER

Not knowing the name of a single hotel in Los Angeles, I asked the studio executive where I should stay. "How about the Chateau Marmont?" he said. "Is that good?" I asked. "Is that good?" he repeated, somewhat stunned. "Well, John Belushi died there."

JAY McINERNEY

Just like those other black holes from outer space, Hollywood is postmodern to this extent: it has no center, only a spreading dead zone of exhaustion, inertia, and brilliant decay.

ARTHUR KROKER

You're no one in Hollywood unless someone wants you dead.

BERNIE BRILLSTEIN

DEATH INC.

The very first movie star was Florence Lawrence. They made money out of her until she was accidentally disfigured on the job, then Hollywood dumped her. Several years later, she killed herself by eating ant paste.

MITCHELL LEISEN

The reason so many people turned up at his [Louis B. Mayer's] funeral is that they wanted to make sure he was dead.

SAMUEL GOLDWYN

In Beverly Hills even death could not dampen curiosity about a movie in the making.

MICHAEL KORDA

I hate funerals. They aren't for the one who's dead, but for the ones who are left and enjoy mourning.

HUMPHREY BOGART

Put my ashes in a box and tell the messenger to bring them to Louis B. Mayer's office with a farewell message from me. Then, when the messenger gets to Louis's desk, I want him to open the box and blow the ashes in the bastard's face.

B.P. SCHULBERG's *final request to his son,*
BUDD SCHULBERG

Last Words —
Some Famous
Hollywood Gravestones

"SHE DID IT THE HARD WAY"
BETTE DAVIS
(Forest Lawn Cemetery, Hollywood Hills)

"GOOD NIGHT SWEET PRINCE
AND FLIGHTS OF ANGELS SING THEE
TO THY REST"
DOUGLAS FAIRBANKS, SENIOR
(Hollywood Memorial Park)

"A GENIUS OF COMEDY
HIS TALENT BROUGHT JOY AND LAUGHTER
TO ALL THE WORLD"
OLIVER HARDY
(Pierce Brothers Valhalla Memorial Park)

"EVERYBODY LOVES SOMEBODY SOMETIME"
DEAN MARTIN
(Westwood Memorial Cemetery)

COLUMBIA / THE KOBAL COLLECTION

"YOU CAN'T HANDLE THE TRUTH!"
A Few Good Men, 1992

FRANKLY, MY DEAR

"WE LIVE TO LOVE YOU MORE EACH DAY"
JAYNE MANSFIELD
(Fairview Cemetery, Pennsylvania)

"TO
YESTERDAY'S COMPANIONSHIP
AND TOMORROW'S REUNION"
RITA HAYWORTH
(Holy Cross Cemetery)

"A MASTER OF COMEDY
HIS GENIUS IN THE ART OF HUMOR
BROUGHT GLADNESS
TO THE WORLD HE LOVED"
STAN LAUREL
(Forest Lawn Cemetery, Hollywood Hills)

Some Important Dates
in the Hollywood Calendar

FEBRUARY 22, 1630 In Massachusetts, popcorn was introduced to the English colonists from the *Mayflower* by Quadequina, brother of Massasoit, the leader of the local Native American tribes.

SEPTEMBER 4, 1781 Los Angeles was founded – as *El Pueblo de Nuestra Señora la Reina de Los Angeles de Porciuncula* ("the village of Our Lady the Queen of the Angels of the Little Portion") – by Felipe de Neve, first Governor of the Californias (then under Spanish rule).

1891–95 This period saw the development of both the cine camera and the projector; with the former, Thomas Alva Edison's Kinetoscope of 1891 (although it was not in fact his own invention) was probably the most influential, but the credit for the first successful film projections rests with the Lumière brothers in France, whose first public screening was in 1895.

FEBRUARY 1, 1893 Edison completed work on the world's first motion-picture studio in West Orange, NJ.

APRIL 2, 1902 The first motion-picture theater was established by Thomas L. Tally as part of a carnival in Los Angeles, CA.

1911 Hollywood's first film studio was opened by the Nestor Company in an old tavern on the corner of Sunset and Gower. Not long thereafter, Cecil B. DeMille and D.W. Griffith began making movies there.

FEBRUARY 8, 1915 Premiere of D.W. Griffith's epic *The Birth of A Nation* in Los Angeles, CA.

1920–30 Proved to be busiest decade in film production, with an average of 800 films a year in contrast to the average of 500 a year in 1990–2000.

1922 Sid Grauman built the Egyptian Theater on Hollywood Boulevard in celebration of the discovery of Tutankhamun's tomb in the same year. Its grand opening is notable for being the occasion of Hollywood's first ever world premiere.

1927 The effective end of the silent era of films came in this year when Warner Brothers produced and debuted *The Jazz Singer*, the first feature-length "talkie" or movie with dialogue. By the end of the decade the film careers of many silent film stars ended due to their voices being unsuitable for the new medium, or due to the fact that their voices didn't match their public image.

1927 The Academy of Motion Picture Arts and Sciences (AMPAS) was founded. Its first awards ceremony was held in 1929.

MAY 18, 1927 Grauman's Chinese Theater opened in Hollywood, California, famed for handprints and footprints of various film stars and celebrities in the cement of the forecourt.

MAY 28, 1929 Premiere of the first all-color talking picture, *On With The Show!* in New York City.

1930s–40s This was the era predominantly referred to as "The Golden Age of Hollywood" by film critics and historians, and considered to be the apex of film history.

FEBRUARY 29, 1939 *Gone With the Wind* won eight Academy Awards, including Best Picture, and went on to gross $192 million worldwide. Best Supporting Actress Hattie McDaniel became the first black actor to win an Oscar.

MAY 1, 1940 Premiere of Orson Welles' *Citizen Kane*. It is perhaps the most highly regarded film in cinematic history, not least for its pioneering role in the development of a huge variety of cinematic techniques and complex non-linear storytelling.

1947 The House Un-American Activities Committee (HUAC) begins to regulate the Hollywood film business, resulting in a purge of the industry. The careers of many of Hollywood's leading lights were ruined when they were blacklisted for communist associations, while some even faced jail sentences. The HUAC's Marcarthyist grip on the industry endured until 1954.

1952 To avoid losing the battle with television, Hollywood counterattacked with 3-D films. The first feature-length 3-D film released was *Bwana Devil*, leading to a flood of other quickly and cheaply made, but sometimes successful, 3-D features.

SEPTEMBER 30, 1955 James Dean, the archetype of a rebellious adolescent, was killed in a car accident aged twenty-six. He had appeared in only three films: *East of Eden* (1955), *Rebel Without a Cause* (1955), and *Giant* (1956), which was released posthumously. Both of his Best Actor Oscar nominations, for *East of Eden* and *Giant*, were also given posthumously.

1959 The chariot race sequence in director William Wyler's Best Picture-winning, wide-screen Technicolor epic blockbuster *Ben-Hur* set the standard for all subsequent action sequences. It was the first film to win eleven Oscars.

AUGUST 5, 1962 Thirty-six-year-old sex symbol Marilyn Monroe died in Los Angeles of an apparent drug overdose. Speculation arose over her associations with President John F. Kennedy and his brother Robert, the Attorney General.

JUNE 12, 1963 The opening of *Cleopatra*, starring Elizabeth Taylor, Rex Harrison, and Richard Burton. This was the most expensive film ever made, but although thought to be one of the biggest flops in film history, it did eventually recover its costs.

1969 The film-maker and cinematographer Gordon Parks directed *The Learning Tree*, and thus became the first black director of a motion picture from a major U.S. studio. This laid the groundwork for Parks's next film – the landmark "blaxploitation" action film *Shaft* (1971) with Richard Roundtree in the title role.

1973 The science-fiction classic *Westworld* was the first movie to make use of "digitized images," a term for what has evolved into CGI (computer-generated imagery) in the present day.

1975 Steven Spielberg's *Jaws* was the first modern '"blockbuster" film to make more than $100 million at the box office in North America, overtaking the previous leaders, *Gone With the Wind* (1939) and *The Sound of Music* (1965).

1977 George Lucas's space adventure *Star Wars*, first released in mid-summer, grossed nearly $200 million, overtaking *Jaws* (1975).

1980 Ronald Reagan became the first movie star to be elected President of the United States.

1995 *Toy Story*, the first totally digital (or computer-generated) feature-length film, was released. It was a joint production by Pixar and the Disney Company, and the first film of Pixar's to go on general release.

1996 Planet Hollywood, a chain of restaurants backed by a number of movie stars including Sylvester Stallone and Arnold Schwarzenegger, became a publicy quoted company. At first its shares rocketed, but within two years its stock fell, and some of the chain's restaurants had to be closed.

1997 James Cameron's *Titanic*, the most expensive film of all time when it was released, became the highest-grossing film in Hollywood history – so far. It won a record-equalling fourteen nominations and eleven Academy Awards, including those for Best Picture and Best Director.

1998 The American Film Institute (AFI) announced its list of the Top 100 American Films of All Time, with Orson Welles's classic *Citizen Kane* (1941) ranked first.

2001 Black actors won in both the Best Actor and Best Actress Oscar categories: Denzel Washington for *Training Day* and Halle Berry for *Monster's Ball*. The latter's Oscar marked the first time a black woman had ever won the award. Denzel Washington became the first black actor to win more than one Oscar.

FRANKLY, MY DEAR

MARCH 2002 Disney closed down its manual-animation department to focus on computer-animated films.

2002 The independently produced romantic comedy *My Big Fat Greek Wedding* became, in percentage terms, the most profitable movie of all time, earning more than $240 million at the box office, against production costs of some $5 million.

2003 In the same year that *Terminator 3: Rise of the Machines* was released its star, Austrian-born actor Arnold Schwarzenegger, was elected Governor of California.

2004 In little over three weeks since its release, *Shrek 2* became the highest-grossing animated film of all time.

2005 It is rumored that *Harry Potter and the Goblet of Fire*, the fourth book in the Harry Potter series of novels, will become the most expensive film ever made – at $170 million – when director Mike Newells brings it to the big screen later in the year.

Bibliography

BOORMAN, JOHN, *Money Into Light – The Emerald Forest: A Diary* (Faber and Faber, 1985)

EVANS, ROBERT, *The Kid Stays in the Picture* (Faber and Faber, 2003)

FITZGERALD, F. SCOTT, *The Crack-Up* (Penguin Books, 1981)

FITZGERALD, F. SCOTT, *The Last Tycoon* (Penguin Books, 1990)

GOLDMAN, WILLIAM, *Which Lie Did I Tell? More Adventures in the Screen Trade* (Bloomsbury, 2000)

GRANT, RICHARD E., *With Nails* (Picador, 1996)

GRAY, SPALDING, *Monster in a Box* (Pan, 1991)

HELLMAN, LILLIAN, *An Unfinished Woman* (Macmillan, 1969)

JACOBS, GEORGE and STADIUM, WILLIAM, *Mr. S – The Last Word on Frank Sinatra* (HarperCollins, 2003)

KEATS, JOHN, *You Might as Well Live – The Life and Times of Dorothy Parker* (Martin Secker & Warburg, 1971)

KORDA, MICHAEL, *Charmed Lives* (Random House, 1979)

LESLEY, COLE, *The Life of Noël Coward* (Jonathan Cape, 1976)

LONG, ROB, *Conversations with My Agent* (Faber and Faber, 1996)

MOOREHEAD, CAROLINE, *Martha Gellhorn – A Life* (Chatto & Windus, 2003)

NIVEN, DAVID, *Bring On The Empty Horses* (Hamish Hamilton, 1975)

WEST, NATHANIEL, *The Day of the Locust* (Penguin, 2001)

YOUNG, TOBY, *How to Lose Friends & Alienate People* (Little Brown and Company, 2001)

Useful Websites

www.thinkexist.com

www.geocities.com

www.corsinet.com

www.historicla.com

www.amusingquotes.com

www.filmsite.org

www.imdb.com